Adventures in Autobumming

Adventures in Autobumming

by
Sinclair Lewis

Omo Press

adolescentium alunt
senectutem oblectant

This book was originally published as a series of articles in the *Saturday Evening Post*.
- "Adventures in Autobumming: Gasoline Gypsies" appeared on December 20, 1919.
- "Adventures in Autobumming: Want a Lift" appeared on December 27, 1919,
- "Adventures in Autobumming: The Great American Frying Pan" appeared on January 2, 1920.

This edition retains inconsistencies that were in the original. For example, the magazine uses both "autohobos" and "autohoboes" as the plural of autohobo. Within just four paragraphs at the beginning of part two, it uses the spellings "globe trotters" and "globe-trotters." In addition, it often uses spellings that are no longer standard, such as "screw driver" and "tooth paste" as two words and "to-day" with a hyphen. It invariably uses "which" where we would now use "that." This book keeps all of the eccentric usages from the original articles.

ISBN: 978-1-941667-16-3
Orignal content in thie edition copyright © 2017 by Omo Press.

Contents

Part 1: Gasoline Gypsies 9

Part 2: Want a Lift 47

Part 3: The Great American Frying Pan 77

Part 1

Gasoline Gypsies

In the good old days, when the happy citizenry were not annoyed by bathtubs, telephones or having enough to eat, any lad could get a deal of innocent pleasure, before he settled down to growing the rest of his beard, out of becoming a pirate and collecting pieces of eight, burning monasteries and torturing old women. Nowadays, fiction writers assure us, there is no chance for a man with courage and imagination to go freely roving the world.

Yet the coming of the gasoline motor, whether in a flivver with a delivery-wagon body or in a tranquil twelve, brought back the age of joyous piracy, with the immense advantage that you do not have to associate with pirates who have the absent-minded habit of cutting your throat. The long-distance motor tourist, swooping down a corkscrew hill into a shining white town of which he has never heard, sliding along a ridge with the fields to westward droning in blue shadows, picking up a wayfarer with new dialect and a new world of interests, is adventurous as any heaving brigantine wallowing all day through changeless seas. He is far more independent—he doesn't have to stay on that uncomfortable and highly undependable medium, the ocean, which is so notoriously ill-suited for walking back after the ship gets wrecked.

Out on the ribbed prairies a lone car really looks like a craft on the circle of the ocean. And as to the practical side of piracy—if the driver doesn't care to attend to that himself he can have it satisfactorily performed by mechanics, hotel keepers and lunch-room cooks along the way.

Making the Get Away Snappy

They who have escaped the touring habit usually ask what is necessary for a long trip. Must they take tents, a pile of extra casings, a seven-foot atlas, a grand piano and vacuum cleaner? Must they be combinations of aviators, deep-sea divers and Dan'l Boones to essay a whole hundred miles from home?

They may take all the equipment they desire, but the fact is that a respectable citizen with a second-hand flivver, who has never driven any car for more than a hundred miles, can start on twenty minutes' notice — ten for his wife to buy a hairnet, ten to tell the maid what she mustn't let the baby do — and with safety and not much trouble drive from Miami to Seattle. He will find repair men every few miles most of the distance; lingerie can be washed in roadside brooks; and from corner to corner of the country are through trails with markers on telephone poles at every turn.

If he wants to camp no one will examine him for insanity. All school-teachers expect to have to crawl between rolls of red comforters and piles of frying pans when they reach their school yards; and any modern farmer would feel lonely if he didn't glance out of the peacock room in the morning and see on the front steps a car that was a combination dining room, nursery, and xylophone.

But the motor trip is to be considered not merely as a vacation but as a duty for all conscientious citizens, for there is nothing which so swiftly and painlessly reduces swellings of the head.

The average citizen never thinks he is an average citizen. Whether he is an insurance man, a fishmonger, a writer of fiction or a trick balloonist, he believes that he is extremely necessary to his business and to his home. He knows at least two people who ask his advice and 'he expects the corner bootblack to call him "Boss." His grocer remembers his favorite brand of tomatoes and the washerwoman is still grateful because of the derby hat he gave her husband year before last. But when he clears the boundary of his county, when he bustles into an unfamiliar garage ten miles away and snaps at the foreman that he wants his differential filled with grease, and he wants it quick, he discovers that news doesn't travel so fast as people say it does—this scoundrel hasn't yet heard the news about Mr. Average Citizen's importance. And after five days out, when the grease has mined into the backs of his hands and his last clean shirt isn't clean, he will be meek when the hoboes along the road grunt at him: "Hey, Billy, gimme a match! Where'd yuh steal de road louse?"

At first he won't like it. He will take hours and hours in telling his wife—sitting beside him and unable to escape without kicking off the switch and crawling out over six suitcases on the running board—that, outside of their home town, people have no friendliness. But after ten days he will revel in being part of the land, of long roads and quiet fields and sloping lovely hills and placid people content to live alone. He will stop worrying about the indubitable ways in which his assistant can ruin his business. He will recover from his ancient irritation about his neighbor's early rising guinea hens. He may even partially forget that a man of his dignity has to act to his own small universe as the representative and image of the Almighty. And when he comes back all men will wonder at his jolly, whimsical modesty—for minutes and minutes they will.

You Aren't a Personage, After All

I had a new car once and a new overcoat; and by request I wasn't wearing the comfortable shoes, but the good-looking ones. I was driving from New York to Chicago with a personage. He was a war correspondent just back from Russia. He had once made love to an Italian princess and he possesses—almost free of debt—an acre of ground near New York, which is the same as owning all of Siberia. We gave ourselves a rating of about ninety h. p. and we looked with pity on all cars which were muddy. Of course we had been through a little mud ourselves and since noon we had washed our hands only when filling the radiator — a heathen custom which consists in spilling half of a can of water on your trousers and the other half on the hood. But nobody could notice those blots on us — no, not possibly.

We came with languid distinction into a small hotel in Ohio. The war correspondent condescended to the landlady in his best Yale and Piccadilly voice: "May we have dinner here?"

She looked us all over. I was prepared to tell her, when she asked, that the new overcoat hadn't really cost a hundred. She smiled gently. She piped: "You boys driving cars through from the factory, or are you private chauffeurs?"

We ate dinner — which wasn't dinner, but supper — with reticence, and we addressed the waitress in tones of humility, and when she snapped at the war correspondent "Tea or coffee, Joe?" he stretched out his paws and purred. We went out and looked, not at the newness and streamlineness of the car but at the mud that clotted the wheels and the general sloppiness of the suitcases in the back; and our hearts were God's little gardens and we completely ceased thinking that we were persons of interest.

And we remained so, because on the next day a peculiarly smeary and recently immigrated Greek bootblack demanded of us, "You fellow drive a truck t'rough?" We knew he was flattering us. He really thought that we were driving a garbage wagon.

On another trip my wife and I were heading westward through a sagebrush desert. As it was after six we were discussing the one subject of real importance to the universe — would we get a decent dinner, and a mattress which wasn't a clay model of the Rocky Mountains, scale one inch to the mile? We stopped a flivver to ask about the hotels ahead.

It was the dirtiest flivver we had yet seen. The hood was so thick with dust-caked grease that it seemed to be cased in gray alpaca. The casings were channeled to the bone. On the running board rode a trunk covered with the flowered-and-stippled tin which, in 1870, was regarded as especially suited to travel and in the tonneau was a rusty stove with frayed gunny sacking thrown over it. The man wore a blue denim shirt, a black felt hat and either he was unable to grow a beard or he had not shaved since starting from Vladivostok. His wife had a visored-and-puckered motor bonnet with eruptions of green veiling.

We stopped and spoke to them gently. We probably had a lot of satisfaction out of being superior and kindly. The vicar's wife permanently relieving poverty by distributing a potato every Whitsuntide had nothing on us for sweetness to the worthy poor.

Many a Wallet is Misjudged

It is true that we were driving a flivver ourselves that trip. But you know how it is. Your flivver is different from all other flivvers. It is smarter and racier and sportier and a lot more powerful. The only reason you have so much difficulty in picking it out from the others at the parking space is because you have dust in your eyes.

So from our sultan of the sand we pleasantly inquired: "What kind of hotel is there in the next town?" The man smiled with the good fellowship of the road and shouted: "Pretty good place." His wife whispered something to him. He stopped. He glanced us over. He scratched his head and went on doubtfully: "I don't know as you'll want to stay there though. It's goldarned expensive."

"How expensive?"

Pityingly—"They want seventy-five cents a night for a room for two!"

As we drove on—

Oh, Burns wouldn't have asked for that giftie of seeing ourselves as others see us if he had ever taken a long motor run. It's valuable for the soul, but it's extremely injurious to the faculty for talking haughtily to office boys and roaring at old bookkeepers. Especially hard on this form of self-ecstasy is contact with strange garage men along the way.

Garage men are—to one who has just taken a tour—

not merely topics of discussion, like matrimony or Lloyd George. They are principles of ethics, like prohibition or the rise in copper.

I have asserted that practically any driver can stand a four-thousand-mile trip. But I must admit that the autohobo should be prepared for these inescapable calamities:

Every third man of whom you ask a direction will say: "Well, I'm a stranger here myself."

The right rear spring will break just after nightfall, when you leave the macadam and hit ten miles of what the man in the last town called "A short stretch of dirt road—might be just a leetle muddy now."

Every day at ten and eleven-thirty A. M., two-sixteen, five-twenty and eleven-fifty-six P. M. you will remember that you mustn't forget to replace the grease cup that has jarred off—and when you get back home it will still be missing.

There is no use of looking to see if the tail-light bulb is burned out. It is.

There is always a better road than the one on the map and if you follow the farmer's advice and take it you will always get lost.

Your partner doesn't want to hear the detailed story of your breakdown—he's waiting to tell you his.

And last and more funereally certain, the garage man will act almost as though he thought you were a fool. There is an interesting psychological reason for that. He does think so.

I have met several hundred apparently sane Sunday afternoon motorists who think they know something about cars. One of them devoted two hours of an invitation drive to repeating clever things he had said to garage men. That is the new way in which citizens give themselves private welcome-home parades. Lunch club conversationalists no longer tell how they caught the big bass or licked the impudent cabman, but how sarcastic they were to the repair man and how superiorly they "taught the fellow a few things about mechanics."

After I had enviously drunk in this amateur's knowledge for two hours he stopped, because the car had sighed gently and stopped also. He listened to the silence, he moistened his finger and held it up to see which way the wind was blowing, he tapped the end of his nose, he took my pliers out of the door pocket and clicked them a few times, he cleaned the glass of the ammeter, then announced: "Trouble is, the engine wasn't getting adequate cooling. I've been noticing all along that the fan belt was loose."

I was grateful. How, I queried, did one tighten the fan belt?

He accumulated a collection of pretzel wrenches, a tire tool, a copper gasket for a cylinder and a Guide to Southern Arkansas; and he attacked the hole in which the fan belt lived. He got the cover off with the loss of only one bolt and jabbed at the belt with his finger. He smiled and vouchsafed—lie is a master of vouchsafing—"It ought to be all right now. Start the motor."

I did—and it didn't. It stopped.

"I'd better go down to the next farmhouse and phone for a repair man," I muttered—It's a wise man who knows when to be discouraged.

But he wasn't in the least discouraged. He looked patronizingly at the scenery—there always is so much scenery on practically all sides when you are stuck on the road. He learnedly tapped the cover of the oil well—it hasn't worked right since. He scraped a little grease off a brass box down there beside the motor which is either the generator, the starter or the insurance policy. He brightened up and said curtly: "The real trouble is in the muffler. It's choked up. Ever had it cleaned out?"

It was an hour later that I telephoned for a garage man. He came out and yawned and inquired: "Why didn't you hook this wire onto the coil? It jarred off.

I don't see how you guys could help noticing it."

My friend did not boast about his knowledge of mechanics again—not for minutes and minutes.

You will see a great deal of garage men, no matter how

much your wife thinks you know. Of course, you may have luck—I know an amateur who drove seventeen hundred miles over corduroy and cut-over roads north and west of Lake Superior without a single puncture, without once having to look at his motor. But again you may be certain of one axiom of repairs: There's always something new that can happen to a car. Whenever you wait in suspense for something you will probably go on for a thousand miles untouched; and whenever you feel that nothing can happen the bearings are just then burning out.

You will discover that seventy per cent of garage employees are honest and capable and that thirty per cent of them ought to be—and recently have been—digging ditches. On the whole, if the typical small American town were all of it as well built and as competent as its tapestry brick garage no one would want to go to the celestial regions—we should be too comfortable here.

In the days of the stage coach returned travelers may have remembered mountains, but to-day it is garage men who punctuate recollections of the voyage. And they differ far more than mountains, all of which have an unimaginative way of sticking up in the air rather like chicken croquettes.

In my own experience there was the garage foreman in the Pennsylvania town near the Alleghanies who patiently soldered a horribly gouged radiator so honestly that it did not leak for twelve thousand miles. He is being advertised gratis by hundreds of drivers from Chambersburg to Zanesville. There is the repair man in St. Paul who is his own boss and staff. He takes in only one car at a time and before he lets it go he tunes it up with all the affectionate eagerness of an owner. People drive thirty and forty miles to beg him to repair their machines. Men like him inspire the autohobo.

But then again—there are garage men who inspire the awed beholder only to direct action. There was the pleasant open-faced youth in the Middle Western town. My car was bucking. Every time it reached twenty-five miles an hour it imitated the heroic steed of the courier in the Civil War play.

Its forefeet shot out in one last mighty leap, its satiny skin shivered convulsively, it whinnied, its noble heart throbbed in almost human response to my despairing cry of "For the union, Nero! We are Sheridan's last hope" — and then it fell dead.

Yes, Something Was Wrong

I was tired of this dramatic performance after about the fourth matinee. I stopped in the next town, though it consisted entirely of a body of unequipped garages surrounded by near-beer signs. I picked out the largest shop — the one that had the free air, only the pump didn't happen to be working to-day.

After the garage man had changed two flivver tires and replaced a broken unbreakable spark plug and telephoned to a girl named Lissenkid, he operated on me. He was sophisticated, he was all of seventeen and he must have learned motor repairing by jerking soda.

Four times I took him joy-riding the length of Main Street — both blocks. The first time he said that the trouble, was that I "gave the boat too much juice, why'n'ell don't you retard the spark?" The fourth time, after Nero had done her celebrated death act in front of cheering spectators gathered at the Boston Drug Store and Silos, the expert admitted that there was something the matter.

He had me stop where the largest possible number of spectators could watch him. He yanked open the hood in that authoritative manner garage men have when they don't know what is the trouble. He looked up and smiled so confidently that I was comforted. Maybe I'd go racing on all of ten miles farther that day.

"You know," he informed me, "there's a lot of these garage men that are hicks just off the farm — never had any experience except tinkering with their tin Lizzies. They're so darn ignorant about ignition that if anything happens they'll always say it's the carburetor. But this time it is the carburetor, sure enough. It needs adjusting."

My carburetor had recently and extensively been adjusted by the service station at the state agency, by a Minneapolis dramatic critic and by the mop salesman who was courting our Swedish maid. But I let him adjust it some more, while at his snappy orders I patiently started the motor and did perfectly meaningless things with the hand throttle and the spark lever. I was so glad that he wasn't the sort who always said it was the carburetor that I agreed with him that "the boat sounds a lot peppier now." I paid him fifty cents and went on my way.

Within half a mile Nero began to die just as regularly and painfully as before. All on my own hook I decided that her—or his—engine was overheated. That's always a safe explanation, because it rarely means anything and doesn't hurt anyone's religious prejudices. It's like climate. Any remarkable climate can be explained by one of three things: Either it's the Gulf Stream or it's the humidity or it's a lie.

When I tried to start the engine again Nero looked up at me with those great beautiful chestnut eyes and expired without even kicking.

After re-re-readjusting the carburetor I telephoned back to the same small town—but to the rival garage. A morose youth came out, looked learnedly into the distributor—and adjusted the carburetor. Then he said he didn't know what the matter was, except that there was something wrong with the carburetor. Either it was the needle valve or the float. He might try taking the float back to town and varnishing it.

Laying Off the Persecuted Carburetor

I suggested that it would be safer if he varnished the needle valve. I persuaded him to haul me ten miles on to a larger town. That was a wonderful drive. Nobody adjusted the carburetor during the whole ten miles. In the larger town the garage man discovered that a wire leading into the coil was broken. Half an hour later I was going on—after the mechanic had adjusted the carburetor back to where it had been when I had started.

The morose youth who had hauled me into town looked on and as I left him he sighed: "Well, that fellow did happen to run onto the real trouble. But just the same, I wish I could of varnished the carburetor float."

"Did you ever varnish one?"

"N-no, but I've heard it was a swell thing to do. Gee, I want to try it once. But somehow I can't get none of these darn hicks in my town to let me try it."

I like to think of the young man in Southern Indiana who on a Sunday afternoon, when I had two simultaneous punctures and only one spare and the garage man in the next town was alone at his shop and unable to drive out in the country, volunteered to help me. He was practically a professional, he said. He knew more 'bout changing casings than any repair man for fourteen miles round.

It took us an hour. Aside from my jacking up the car, removing the two rims, prying the rims open, yanking off the casings, putting in the new tubes, getting the casings back and doing a quarter of the hand pumping— in the August sun and dust—my rescuer did the whole thing. The small items mentioned, along with the general blue-printing and management, fell to me.

"How much'll it be?" I inquired at the end. I felt proud and generous. I was willing to give him a quarter.

"We'el, let's see—'n'our; say 'n'our and a quarter—I guess it's worth about two dollars."

But the worst garage man I ever encountered was the night attendant at a back-alley shop in a small city in Ohio. I had had a long and bumpy day's ride. I slid into the city so tired that it was hard to climb out of the seat. I weaved into the office of the largest hotel, feebly registered and inquired for the nearest garage.

All I wanted from that garage was the privilege of paying fifty cents to a dollar for enough space in which to leave the car till morning and the boon of wearily driving my car into one of the many empty stalls without troubling the attendant. I rumbled drowsily in and waited for the attendant to tell me where he wanted me to put the car. He was working on a local machine. He didn't lift his head. He was a thick-shouldered, fist-jawed, red-eyed, blackly unshaven man, and he was growling at the customer: "Why the devil don't you take off your kid gloves and put a little oil in her now and then?" He said it in a voice like an emery wheel, and the local motorist, instead of going right out and organizing a lynching party of his neighbors, took it meekly.

I called to the garage man: "Where shall I put my car?"

He ignored me. He got into the other car and drove it outside under an arc light.

Three times he came back into the garage for tools; three times I asked him which stall I should take. Though he passed me, not ten feet away, he ignored me still. I was to wait till he had time to say the five words I wanted.

I crawled out of the car, wabbled outside and demanded: "Would it hurt you to answer me? Do you want this car in here to-night or don't you?"

He was not accustomed to such impudence from low customers. He found time to speak for the first time. He bellowed: "I don't care a damn whether you put your improperly descended car in or not. See? Get the hell out of here."

If I had been built like Jim Jeffries I should have given him the one logical answer, the one answer he could have understood. But he could have beaten me with his little finger — and he was waiting and hoping for that pleasure. I backed my car out, so tired and furious that my foot was trembling on the clutch, and in my blindness I almost hit the fender of a car parked across the street.

My friend had his chance — and he had plenty of time for ardent speech now, though he had not finished the repairing. He came over bawling that he'd show me — he'd get me — deliberately smashing people's cars — tryin' to, anyway — he'd see I was pinched — he'd take my number.

And I had no gun with me!

He bellowed so that half a dozen firemen came out of the near-by fire house and looked on mildly. He made much of flashing an electric torch over my number plate, of pretending to note down my number on a stray and excessively dirty repair-order blank. I hoped that he would really summon a policeman. He didn't.

The Blacklist of Autohobodom

I got the car to the street beside the hotel—where I left it all night—and I started on the trail. I knew that the night attendant could not be the owner of the place. Even the surliest owners do not take quite so much pains to escape being paid for unused space. I found that the owner was also the proprietor of a not-very-savory cigar stand and pool room. Of course he personally could not stay at his garage—he had to show off his checked vest and his skill at pool.

I told my story. He grunted: "Fellow hadn't ought to talked to you like that. Probably drunk again. Guess I'll have to speak to him about it."

It wasn't till I reached New York that I got even. I ought to pretend that I was merely looking for justice and protection to fellow motorists who might make the error of stopping at that hotel and being sent to that garage, but I wasn't. I was looking for homicide and satisfaction. I gave up my first earnest idea of going back there with a four-wheel-drive, two-ton prize fighter as passenger and returning to the garage at night. In New York I called on an official of the automobile association, and gave him the name of the Ohio town, the hotel and the garage.

"I've heard other complaints about that town—and there's good towns ten or fifteen miles on either side of it. I'll see that all tourists are advised to keep right on through it hereafter," said the official.

I wonder how many thousands of dollars the hotels and restaurants and garages of that town, good and bad, have lost in the two years since then? I wonder why the good ones tolerate and share the blame of the bad ones? I wonder why the owner hadn't the honesty to close the garage at night if the only attendant he could offer the public was a drunken thug?

It is unfortunate that trouble is more dramatic than happiness; that an autohobo better remembers the few garage men who have been hogs than the hundreds who have made motoring agreeable by competent repairs, by looking cheerful as they turned the handle of the gasoline pump or by giving road directions. But even if they are forgotten, the competent garage man may be glad to know that they are not being evilly gossiped about by thousands of motorists; that they haven't active enemies who take pleasure in trying to steer people away from their shops.

It is the duty of every touring motorist to kick as effectively as he can about every garage where he has dishonest or uncivil treatment. There is in Washington, D. C., an organization of local, motorists which members to report, with proofs, all complaints against garages, gas stations or dealers in automobile supplies, and it investigates—and acts.

And it is the duty of every garage man who prides himself on being independent and "not takin' nothin' off nobody" to ask if just possibly he isn't simply an offensive specimen of what he would call a roughneck.

In a California town, where all of us were meek to the one garage man, I finally exploded and asked him if he—a boy of twenty—realized that he talked to his customers as though they were panhandlers. Then I took my car away from there and drove it five miles off for some rather expensive overhauling.

The boy hunted me up and wailed that he didn't know he had been rude; that he couldn't possibly have been rude. When I repeated what other owners had recently said about him he came near to crying. I saw then how unconscious is most gruffness. But I also saw that if large numbers of autohoboes would lose their fear of seeming priggish and roar every time they were mistreated there would be a quick change in motor manners.

Until the millennium when the boors are wakened to their own rudeness and become little sunbeams—and that may take several months—I recommend to ex-service men who want to keep in military training that they go touring and carry a machine gun.

They will need it for only about one garage man in forty, but for the fortieth — unless he hears the warning and actually attaches it to himself instead of to the mechanic across the street — the machine gun will be handy and appropriate.

It was not discourtesy but a comedy of irritations — the collision and the delay between Wheeling and Columbus. I was heading from New York to the Mississippi with a youngster, a college senior, as my guest. Hoping to make Columbus for the night, we kept on through the darkness over a narrow but excellent cement road. Jack was driving. Being young, he still believed that a motor car is like an aeroplane — you can go as fast as you want to wherever you want, and if another car unexpectedly shows up just in front you can depress the elevating plane and skim over it. My own experience indicates that this aviation theory of motoring is an error.

Etiquette in Accidents

Jack kept to the center of the narrow road. Ahead of us was a rise of ground and the glow behind it indicated the headlights of an approaching car. I took it for granted that he saw the glow and was going to take to the right to avoid being dazzled. Taking things for granted keeps the morgue filled.

But as it was my car I did interfere with the pilot to the extent of suggesting, "Better stay over — you're three feet from the edge."

I was just saying it when everything happened at once. There was a blam, a sound of glass breaking, not much of a jar, then silence so deep that we could not help noticing the crickets in the deep Ohio cornfield by the road. Incidentally we noticed that we seemed to have smashed into another vehicle. I had wondered what my sensations would be in a thumping accident and now I knew. They were an interesting nothing at all. My only improving and moral reflection was: "Confound it, now I'll be delayed again — maybe for a whole day."

I climbed out and not till then did I have the dramatic satisfaction of beginning to be scared. I realized that there had been damages; that the other car was a flivver; that we had torn away one of its fenders and part of a running board, crushed a light, twisted the front axle and turned a wheel into splinters of wood and rubber.

What they had done to us I could not see — their lights were out.

From the flivver erupted four furious gentlemen, all colored. They closed on me and shrieked: "You got to pay for our car. It was your fault. We was way over on our side of the road. We wasn't running but twelve miles an hour. It was your fault. You got to pay for —"

"Sure, I'll pay for it," I protested as often as I had the chance.

I didn't know then how suspiciously I was acting. I have since learned the etiquette and good form of accident. Even if you run into a parked car with its lights on it is the correct thing to clamor that a dog startled you; that at great self-sacrifice you saved the lives of two prattling babes whose immediate disappearance and subsequent absence you simply can't understand; that the other man's tail light prevented your brakes from taking hold; and that, anyway, he was parked on the wrong side of the street and had since moved over. By and by, after a good noisy time has been had by all and both of you have chanted the anthem, "You'll pay for my car," in chorus and lawyers have been ardently spoken of, you settle for two-thirds of the damages and go on scowling and feeling happy.

But I was so amenable that they were sure I was lying.

"You better ante right up. We was way over on our side."

"All right!' All right ! I'll pay!"

"Yas, you bet you will! Mose, you better go telephone for our lawyer, less'n he gets away 'thout paying."

Of course I was heroic and all that, and very haughty, and awed them with a glittering eye, only it was so dark that they didn't see the eye. The four of them didn't weigh more than seven hundred and twenty pounds together. They meant, I gathered, that they desired me to pay for their car.

Nationalizing the Smashup

I separated the leader from his oratory, led him to my car and demanded: "Will you tell me how I'm going to get away?"

In the light of an electric torch I showed him that my car had lost a wheel, bent the front axle, and crumpled a fender.

"Yassuh, I guess that's right. But you got to pay for the whole thing," he said quite pleasantly.

By now, at night, on a country road half a mile from any farmhouse and a mile from the nearest settlement, a crowd of twenty had assembled and they stood in an admiring circle, ever so grateful to me for having gone out for rustic uplift and provided all this wholesome amusement.

There was one of the crowd whom I shall always remember as original. He did not say "What did you do? Hit the Lizzie?" He said, "Hit the tin Liz, eh?" He saw right away how it was, so I got hold of him and asked about telephones and garages. I sent Jack to telephone to both the flivver garage and the agency for my brand of car in a town—oh, call it Sodom.

There was a dance at a farmhouse down the road and the dancers came to giggle at my show. They averaged seventeen in age and hysterical in delight. They had never seen anything funnier than my twisted axle. I turned upon them like a tigress—my car and the flivver being the imperiled cubs. I thought that I was being impressive as I explained that this was not vaudeville but an unfortunate and strictly private accident.

As the months go by I become more certain that I must have been even funnier than the wreck. I remember the delighted applause when I finished being lofty and the dancers tumbled into their cars.

Now arrived noisily and very competently the driver of the jitney plying between the near-by settlement and Sodom. He took charge at once. He was the first spectator to understand without explanations that somebody might easily have run into somebody else round here recently. The four colored gentlemen broke into a Gregorian chant again and laughingly admitted that they had been on their side of the road and this fellow pays for our car.

The jitney driver stormed: "Sure, he'll pay! I'll drive you to town and he'll have the flivver agent bring your car in tomorrow. Heh? Certainly I know him. He's good for it. Shut up or I'll testify you hit him!"

Oh, blessed golden liar! He had never seen me before. He drove my beloved wreckmates away, the crowd gloomily gave up hope that there would be a fight or another wreck and I was left in sweet peace. By repeatedly looking at my car with the electric torch, but suddenly leaping at it with the light and catching it unawares, I was at last convinced that there was no doubt about it—the axle was bent and I would not be going on to Columbus that night.

Jack returned to say that the Sodom agent for my car was already on his way. Then the real work began. I had to assure Jack that his running into the flivver didn't matter at all, when the one thing I really knew was that I wanted to bite him. I have never had a chance to be so noble and forgiving. And Jack stood it. He didn't tell me to go to the devil—that is, not for some time.

In an hour a scurry of lights, a ye-a-ow of a horn, the shrieking of brakes announced the coming of my garage man from Sodom. He was a large-mustached, brisk person. He leaped out, followed by his dark, dour little assistant. Not even speaking to me, he got busy, jacking up my car, taking off the battered wheel.

"This is fine!" I exulted. "Here is a real repair man. Look at him! Why, we'll get new parts from Columbus and be on our way by to-morrow noon."

That was on Tuesday evening.

Yes, certainly. To-morrow morning the garage man would phone into Columbus for a new wheel and fender. He'd take the axle to a blacksmith to be straightened. He'd have me out of this by to-morrow evening, sure pop. S'long ! Good luck!

They were gone with a snort from the exhaust. Night was tranquil about the scenes of the battle of Jutland and I was unbothered—except by figuring up how much all this was going to cost. Sometimes I made it a hundred dollars, but mostly—till I got sleepy—I could keep it down to sixty.

I slept in the back of my car, while poor silent Jack crept off to a straw stack. I wish to record for all autohoboes that the back seat of a touring car is a perfectly good place for a six-footer to sleep, provided he merely has his legs amputated at the knees.

At two or six in the morning I was wakened by the light of a car pouring into my protesting eyes. It was a truck and the driver had come to anchor while he looked over the free exhibit. When he had completely examined both cars he came to me and sprayed the light of his torch on me in my vest-pocket bed with my knees snugly fitted beside my ears. He glowered and said as though he was daring me to deny it: "There's been a smash-up."

"The deuce there has!" I marveled.

R. D. S. C. for the Mechanic

At nine the flivver wrecking crew arrived and by noon they had our opponent somewhat better than new. I watched the miracle of repairing. You know how it goes. Nothing ever fits. The mechanic spends all his time taking off whatever he has just put on, shaking his head and sighing: "No, that doesn't seem to do the trick.

Guess I'll try—" Yet somehow he gets out the car.

They took the flivver away after charging me fifty-six dollars for parts and time. It was my first installment on the payment for the pleasure of having almost been lynched. At noon my own garage man came back with my axle straightened and a temporarily borrowed wheel. He was my big brother, guardian, boss, favorite author and candidate for president. I beamed on him in boyish faith and chirruped: "Well, we going to get on our way to-night? What did Columbus say? Have they shipped the parts? Ought to be here this afternoon."

Oh, Columbus? Oh, Columbus didn't have any parts! But, rats, that didn't matter! He had telephoned to Cincinnati for the parts. He'd have me on the road by to-morrow noon — oh, absolutely!

This was Wednesday noon.

It was good to deal with a man who got things done like that. I stood about cherubically while he and his silent little mechanic put back the axle and screwed on the wheel they had borrowed. The assistant didn't give me any words of cheer and confidence. He didn't have time. He had to do the work, for it proved that though my tutelary garage man was a marvel of optimism; financial organization, salesmanship and fine flushed oratory he did have one fault — he didn't know a thing about motor cars. He whispered to his assistant to ask what to do next, then did it publicly and with a flourish, and the hearts of all beholders were made glad and sang together at the spectacle of efficiency and power.

He towed the disabled car and ourselves into Sodom. Jack and I were hungry. We had had two sandwiches during the day. Our father, guide and friend dusted his hands, yearned upon us and said invitingly: "Well, I'm going home and see if mother can't shake up something to eat. You boys like a little supper?"

Oh, this was the king of hosts! We chorused "Sure," and looked upon him filially and were ready to follow him.

"Well, you'll find a pretty good restaurant across the street. See you later, boys."

And it was a pretty good restaurant. It was a sawed-off lunch counter at the front of a pool parlor. The menu consisted of fried eggs, boiled eggs, ham sandwiches,

Hamburger sandwiches, coffee; and the ham sandwiches tasted like the boiled eggs, the coffee like the Hamburgers and the salt and pepper like nothing whatever. During my six meals the menu was changed only once. That was when they were out of ham sandwiches.

We dined modestly, then took the train into Columbus and had something to eat.

Next morning—Thursday—we were wise. The garage man had said he'd have the car out by noon, but we knew—oh, we knew! We were convinced that he would not have it ready till midafternoon. We spent the morning in avoiding the roving Hamburger sandwich, and scientists may be interested to know that we found the movies to be the safest refuge from this insidious and pandemic pest. We returned to Sodom at four. We burst into the garage tingling with hope and found the car—it was there, all nice and safe, and merely lacked a wheel, a fender and a few hours' adjustment of the steering gear. Our lord, the garage man, hailed us.

"Well, boys, seems like the parts ain't showed up yet. Expect 'em on every train. Fact is, I found Cincinnati was out, too, so I phoned to Detroit."

That was Thursday afternoon.

The parts arrived Monday morning.

Jack had to go on. I faced Sodom alone.

During the years that followed, while golden summer succeeded to spring and vice versa, and our heroine developed from the little girl we once knew into a broad-browed, and strikingly handsome young woman, I spent Thursday to Monday in meeting trains, peering into express cars, not getting the parts and going back to explore the town. It was a work of supererogation. A two-month-old kitten could have seen enough of Sodom in one hour. The population was four hundred and the only points of interest for a Seeing Sodom Car—which would have been a wheelbarrow—were the brickyard, the new bungalow with cement Corinthian columns and an Aztec door, and the theological debate in front of the drug store.

Pool as a Side Dish

The debaters were the town agnostic and the druggist, who was the Sunday-school superintendent but wanted it known that he was a good sport and shook a wicked cue at the pool parlor. The discussion had now continued for ten years and had resulted in the following conclusions:

"Now hold your horses! Keep your shirt on! Look here! What you say may all be true. I'm willing to admit there's a lot of people that's prejudiced in their views and maybe they don't always live up to their theories, but trouble is with you fellows you don't never stop and consider the effect on other folks. 'Sall right for you and me to think what we like, but let me tell you right here, they ain't everybody can think for themselves, like you and me."

I have never seen this so clearly put though just now I cannot remember whether it was the superintendent or the town agnostic who said it.

Whenever I became too hungry to sit in—or on—the press box and report the conference, l went to eat another fried egg and watch the pool players. But I have never yet learned how many strikes the batter gets in pool or why it is that the pitcher always stands back and rubs the small end of his bat with a piece of cuttlefish.

The rest of the time I prowled through the garage.

There is something about watching a mechanician work which paralyzes time. At first you are brisk; you will learn something; you will study the repair man's system of tracing ignition trouble. But as he never does anything but look under the cowl and grunt "Where the deuce is the fuses in this car?" you fail to get more than half an hour killed. Then you explore. In all garages, in all states, you look over, and one by one you disapprove of the doctor's coupe, the barber's sporty four-passenger roadster, the grocer's delivery wagon, the real-estate man's ancient but powerful six for which he wouldn't take fifteen hundred dollars—unless somebody offered it—and you end up by pensively kicking the car which was horribly smashed six years ago come Shrove Tuesday and which the shop foreman has for six years intended to rebuild as soon as he gets time.

You stroll along the workbench and get your fingers dirty. You inspect a new kind of wrench and lay it down with dignity, because the cynical garage man is looking at you and you think he thinks you are going to steal it. He does. And how do we know but what —

You haughtily leave him and go into the office and read the library, which consists of one newspaper two days old, one tire company's house organ, a red-bound golden blazoned catalogue of motor accessories, and one copy of a magazine devoted to mechanical novelties — diagrams of the monorail that is going to revolutionize transportation and of the device for catching submarines in a vacuum cleaner. After half an hour with all these masterpieces of fiction it is surprising with what appetite you can eat a Hamburger sandwich.

These were the dissipations of my stay in Sodom. My real business was meeting Number 7, Number 623 and Number 41 at the station to see if the parts for my car were aboard — running beside the express car, peering in at all large bundles that might contain a wheel and a fender, seeing the express agent hand down to the depot agent nothing but a dog collar and two large Manila envelopes and watching the train dustily puff away.

Sodom's Social Barriers

I have indicated that motoring is a corrective of self-opinion. The stay in Sodom was. Though the restaurant proprietor unbent so far as to inform me that his "old woman had a fierce grouch this morning," though the religious conference looked only mildly bored when I joined it, yet a realization of my supreme unimportance to Sodom crept into my bones. I walked the streets demurely and hoped that some dog, some honored local dog, would wag its tail at me.

I had been several years past thirty when I arrived in Sodom, but after three days of being called "Bub" and "My boy" and "Billy" I was demoted to a timorous and unworldly eighteen. My ambition was to be socially recognized and invited to a regular meal at the garage man's house. That ambition is, to date, unsatisfied. It must be thrilling to move in exalted social sets and hear the repartee and chit chat and beaux arts and quod ests and everything, and eat apple sauce and creamed chipped beef instead of Hamburger sandwiches.

On Monday morning, when I had reached sixteen years of age, the parts arrived, were attached and the white road lay open before me; and never again in all my touring could I possibly have the slightest trouble.

I tried out the car. It steered rather hard. The youthful mechanic said patronizingly: "Oh, that'll loosen up in just a coupla miles."

Never did an ancient eager for news of his future more greedily assist a backstreet clairvoyant to deceive him than I assisted this mechanical faith healer. I paid eighty-eight dollars for the parts and the labor. The royal garage man thundered farewell and I told him that he had been my rescuer, my preserver, my controller of destiny. I gayly boomed on toward Columbus.

The car could be steered only by bracing my feet, getting a grip on the wheel and yanking it. I made a hundred and forty miles before I sagged into bed, but next morning my hands were raw. And, ten miles from Lima—constantly, unconsciously, a driver makes tiny corrective movements of the wheel to keep the car in the road. But so stiff was the steering that this time before I could correct the course I discovered that the car wasn't on the road at all but amazingly and incredibly down in a ditch and flourishingly heading for a barbed-wire fence. I stopped in time, but I sat in the ditch and wondered whether the steering gear would loosen up before I got killed. It seemed improbable. But I'd be hanged if I'd waste any more time on another repair man. Never again! No, sir!

So in Lima I went to another repair man. I had been convinced that whatever in life might be fallible, the one Rock of Ages was the integrity of the ruddy-voiced garage man of Sodom and his mechanic. In the Lima machine shop I found that the axle—oh, yes, the Sodom blacksmith had straightened it all right, only he hadn't straightened it so that the two halves were anything alike.

The restraightening took one more day and seventeen more dollars. In all, including expenses while waiting, it cost me one hundred and seventy-six dollars to discover that accidents were not thrilling and that I had no great message or mission for the community of Sodom.

But I did get to Minneapolis with only four more stops to have garage men rerepair things that had been repaired at Sodom.

I have met a few major generals, peers and senators; a few famous surgeons and capitalists and aviators and explorers; but I have never met so lordly and soul-satisfying a presence as that paternal garage man of Sodom, nor anyone who so ably convinced me that large parts of the universe may still go on after I have passed. He looked upon me redly and was bored and told me to run along and play and I went. The jokes that had got me a hand at the club fell smashed before his desk, and the theories of government which I had been thinking of letting the President have never got farther with the garage man than a timorous "Say, cap'n, did you ever stop and think —"

He may have turned out incompetent repairs, but as a corrector of destinies he is recommended to all my fellow autohoboes.

The joys of the road, the zest of travel intensified because you yourself are guide and you wait neither for train nor tide—that exhilaration so far outweighs discomforts that once you have made a long motor trip through new lands the first dry road of every coming spring will coax you out to Northern forest, Western prairies, Southern mountains or Eastern streets. It is not at all because they are so memorable as the long, hazy days of perfect driving but because there is in them more of freakish amusement that I recall more mishaps than bright days.

You may be prepared for unfamiliar beauty—but you

must be prepared for trouble; not only for breakdowns and tedious waits, but also for bad roads—sand, mud, ruts, bridges out and the way blocked by a traction engine, ten miles of road so repaired by heaping dirt in the center that you crawl along with one wheel three feet lower than the other. You must be ready for heat, dust, rain that will seep in through side curtains, weariness so profound that it will be too much trouble to lace up the top eyelet of your boots in the morning, and that most sensational of all calamities—arguments with your passenger.

Pronged Forks of Infelicity

These arguments will make you regard the other casualties as mere frolicsome incidents. They are the most damaging thing that can occur—because they will reveal to you that the masculine logic and lucidity of which you have always been so proud have been merely blustering and quick exits.

Your passenger is probably your wife and she has much to endure. In normal times she is comfortably rid of you while you are at the office or out playing golf; but on tour she has twenty-four hours a day in which to discover how inexact are your opinions.

The man back there in the last town has told you to take the left-hand turn at the fork and you naturally have taken the right. Your passenger objects.

"He said to go to the left."

"Nonsense! He said right."

You illustrate with an abrupt, virile gesture. Enough of this needless chatter.

"Oh, please! You almost knocked my hat off."

"Well, I didn't knock it off, and anyway—why did you wear that hat? Blow off in the first high wind"

"Would you mind noticing that meanwhile we are on the wrong road and getting farther and farther away from the fork?"

"Now — see — here! We're heading southwestward, aren't we? There's the sun. Well then, this is correct!"

"But the map shows a jog. We ought to go north."

"Oh, those maps are crazy! They just guess at them. I suppose if you wanted to go to San Antonio you'd start for Montreal!"

"No, I'd stop and ask some directions."

"Oh — these fellows don't know anything about the road."

"My dear, can you explain to me the reason why no man ever likes to ask directions? I suppose it would be a reflection on his masculine omniscience!"

"All right! All right! I'll stop and ask! Then I hope you'll be satisfied that I'm right!"

Silence. Presently from passenger: "Why didn't you ask one of those two men?"

"I only noticed one man. We haven't been by but one — and he didn't look like any intellectual giant."

"Slow down. There's a team in that barnyard."

"Good heavens, I was just slowing down! What did you think I was doing? Say, uh, hey! Say, is this the right road for Bottleville?"

The farmer looks sorry for you and regrets: "No, I'm afraid you took the wrong turn back at the fork."

"Yuh, I kind of thought maybe this was wrong. Much 'bliged."

Eschew a Motorwise Wife

The road is narrow and you back and fill seven times before you turn, and once because you are an infallible male and you'll be hanged if you'll ask her to look back and see how much room you have — and why doesn't she think of doing it without being asked, anyway? — you drop into the ditch and have to crawl out on low. Then you return to the fork.

All this time the passenger hasn't said a word. She hasn't

needed to. Every bird on the barbed-wire fence, every frog in the slew, even the humming telegraph wire, has been twanging "I tolllllld you soooooo."

If you are a man without wisdom you wail: "Well; go on, say it!" But if you are of the blessed you grin at her and congratulate her on her new hat.

Before being taken on a motor tour wives who themselves drive should be anesthetized and all knowledge of motors removed. For if they know anything about the game it is so hard to explain to them why when you are trying to pass a car on the hill and suddenly see another car bearing down you first step on the accelerator instead of the brake, then retard the spark, yank the gear lever into neutral, grindingly try to get it into reverse or low or anything that is handy, sound the horn, step on the gas again, finally get into second—and then kill the motor. So dangerous a thing is a little knowledge that in such cases women have been known to doubt your having perfect reasons for all those clever maneuvers.

Motoring is the real test of marriage. After a week of it you either stop and get a divorce, or else-free from telephone calls and neighbors and dressing for dinner, slipping past fields blue with flax and ringing with meadow larks in the fresh morning—you discover again the girl you used to know.

Even without searching for them, you are certain to find odd, unbelievable places on any long trip.

I remember Southern ferries where you help the ferryman to pole your way across the yellow stream; Western fords where you splash through a torrent and instantly shoot up a mountain rise; Tennessee cabins as aboriginal as in the days of Dan'l Boone; St. Ignatius, that Alpine town with unmistakably Italian convent and mission tower, which nevertheless is in Montana; old Rockbridge Alum Springs, where once the flower of Virginia and the Carolinas rode and danced and made love; young Mennonites in Pennsylvania with silky chin whiskers, grotesque under their pink cheeks;

a Shaker settlement of vast barns in a valley between Albany and Pittsfield; a road between Bemidji and Duluth through pines impressive as columns of an Egyptian temple, broken only by infrequent clearings where Indians looked up from cultivating corn to hold up a stolid arm in greeting; cowpunchers riding range in Oregon—in chaps even today; the climb up out of Pittsburgh like crawling up the side of a smoking caldron.

The other day, when we were thinking of nothing but Chicago ahead, we drove into Zion City and discovered that the followers of the forgotten Dowie are very much existent. Zion City remains pure. Not liquor alone, but oysters, pork, profanity, doctors and all forms of tobacco are still forbidden. But when I saw that they had a garage I could not believe that the anti-swearing ordinance applied to it. Automobiles are descended from mules and should be so addressed. I asked one of the repair men about it. Was he of the faith? Oh, yes, he had been cured of a toothache by the faith. Well, then, as driver to driver, was it true that there was no cussing in the garage?

It was! He'd worked there a year and he hadn't heard a single cuss word. Not one!

I marveled, and while I marveled he drove a car between two others with half an inch to spare on either side. He did not swear. All he remarked to his car was: "You dinged Siwash," "You blinking son of trouble" and "There, by fiddle, I'll show you, lam blast you!"

It was so improving to get away from the vulgar worldly atmosphere of profanity. I had passed Zion City a dozen times on the train, but if I had not been motoring I should never yet have chanced to stop there and get improved like that.

But odder than any religious colony was the river in the road.

We started south and east of Minneapolis after the Minnesota River had been flooding. Our normal way followed the river. As we approached it we saw a large sign, "Road Under Water." So naturally we kept on. It had the same effect as the no-smoking sign in a garage, which invariably causes all beholders, including the man who put it up, to reach for the cigarettes.

A quarter of a mile on we discovered three cars stopped and the occupants inspecting a stream across the road, where the flood had cut through, gravel to mud. Huh! I wasn't one to be scared by a little water. Besides, there were wheel marks on the opposite side of the cut, showing that someone had crossed. Oh, I knew, I knew!

I informed the awed populace: "I'll try it if you'll wait and pull me out if I get stuck."

Oh, yes, indeed they would. They would stay by me till Der Tag. Long live our leader brave!

I drove cheerfully into the gash in the road, splashed through with water above the running board—and stopped. Now I knew what had made those wheel marks on the farther side. Other goats had also spent the springtide hours in trying to get out while their wheels spun round and round and made inviting marks in the soft mud of the farther bank.

A Modern Arabian Fadeaway

I looked back. Two of the cars that had been going to help me out were already headed due north and keeping going. But the driver of the third was loyal—and probably foolish.

Trying to remain dignified, I peeled off my shoes and socks and rolled up my trousers. And let me right here inform the world of science that, judging by photographs taken of the scene, it is not possible for a tall lank male to look dignified when his trousers are bunchily rolled up over his prominent knees. I got out and I got wet. I hitched a steel towing wire to the back axle and handed it to the man ashore and his car tried to pull me out backward.

It didn't.

We both had a smoke and assured each other that

"trouble is, don't get any traction in the mud—better put some stones and brush behind the wheels."

The stones were heavy, but they were first-class marksmen. Every time they dropped they got us in the eye with a spurt of mud. At last we straightened up, rubbed our backs as the unfortunate sufferer does in the advertisements of the rheumatism cure, glanced proudly at our engineering and tried again and—oh, I told him he might as well go on and leave me. He did—with speed. And my car remained in a river, entirely surrounded by landscape and water.

My passenger crawled out on the hack fender, leaped ashore and walked to the nearest farmhouse, with the suggestion that they could make all of a couple of dollars by hauling us out. I sat in the car and felt like an outdoor person and a hero—which is the chief reason why indoor typewriter-pounding people, such as writers and shipping clerks and the President, like to go motoring.

It was the passenger who had the trouble. When she came brightly up to the farmhouse and made her generous offer they almost set the dog on her. They told her that we were the twenty-seventh pair of idiots who during three days had been too wise to heed signs and had with some difficulty managed to get themselves mired. Three days ago they had spent an afternoon in getting out one big car. They had received five dollars for it—and the rain had come and they had lost one hundred dollars worth of hay.

It was sometime in the evening when two members of a road gang took three minutes to haul us out and briefly accepted five dollars. By driving rapidly we were able a little later in the evening to be—at midnight—exactly as far ahead as we had been at noon—when we had started. But it was worth it. If you wish to be free from conventions and tradition and flattery, sit in a car apparently intended for dry-land transportation, look out at the muddy traces of a flood and contemplate your lack of wisdom. There is no need of going to a Himalayan mountain or of consorting with yogis in yellow shirts to attain meditation and the silences and a good tan.

The Fallacy of Good Roads

More weighty than garage man, more significant to the autohobo than scenery, are the roads. So much has, been said about the good-roads movement that most people vaguely feel that the country is now a network of perfect highways, and because of that belief they are bored by further propaganda and infuriated by further taxes. The Farmers — the very people who in their isolation are most aided by good roads — many of them still believe that a highway bond proposal is "a graft for the sole benefit of city joy riders." The quotation is neither imaginary nor ancient. It appeared in 1919 in a Middle Western farm paper. The paper did not explain whether there was also an objection to vegetables, grain and cream going joy-riding into town.

The movement hasn't yet even begun and will not be under way till there is a grid of hard-surfaced and perfectly maintained pikes not more than twenty miles apart all over the country. While manufacturers are doing their intense best to produce perfect tires, batteries, transmission, body comfort, and the rest, their efforts are almost annihilated by the bad roads of the country. Not till every taxpayer admits that if his own roads are bad he cannot expect boulevards in the next county will let the manufacturers have a chance to show what cars can be.

I have never found an interstate highway, not even the most famous of them, which, did not have sections which would have been a disgrace to the Balkan States in A.D. 1600.

I have never driven in a state that did not have its share of bad roads — possibly excepting Rhode Island and Connecticut. Even California, New York, Pennsylvania and Massachusetts, despite their fame for highways and the example they set the rest of the country, have their vile stretches. And as to the rest of them, even on their through, interstate, main highways —

In the state of Washington I have found deep ruts covered with a foot of sifted dust, so that they looked smooth as a beach — and invited the driver to break springs. In Montana and Idaho there were short, sharp ascents, heartbreaking to climb and dangerous to descend; and there were pitches equally uncomfortable and even rougher in Wisconsin on the highroad between La Crosse and Madison. I have found mud in Minnesota, Iowa and North Dakota; mud and temper-jarring miles on miles of bumpy old decayed macadam in Ohio and Illinois and Indiana. In Kentucky there were—on an important pike—cobbles as rough as a medieval street; and in Northern Tennessee was a mountain climb as steep and twisty as anything in the Rockies, with a road coating of sharp flints guaranteed to take five hundred miles' wear out of a casing in one mile. I have been mired down in Virginia mud. I have been jarred to pieces on famous interurban highways in Maryland, Delaware, New Jersey and Oregon. In Nebraska there were hill roads almost unclimbable except during two dry months of summer; and in Georgia and all its neighbor states I have seen trunk highways that were trails of brush and wet red dirt.

If local taxpayers in every state will admit that, though they personally have learned to dodge the big rock two miles out and the sink hole a mile beyond, strangers will not necessarily find those features amusing, then perhaps we may some day begin to have a system of highways. We have the best motor cars in the world, and some of the worst. Oh, let's be patriotic!

Besides, come to think of it, while the state next to yours has bad roads, yours never has—and you can prove it.

Once in a story, though I hymned the lakes and glorious fields and friendly hills of a certain state, I did depict a character as stuck in the mud. I shortly realized that it would have been more popular to have written scandal about the pastors of the state and to have assassinated the governor. The state was at the time discussing a huge bond issue for—oh, surely not for improving the roads, because it was immediately proved to me that all the roads in the state were already perfect. Indignant persons wrote to the misguided editor who had taken the story. One of the best newspapers of the state officially announced in an editorial that though possibly I hadn't meant to lie yet certainly I had been grievously misinformed by evil persons. It's notorious, anyway, that all fiction writers stay at home in bobbed-haired literary colonies and get a mysterious substance called local color from persons who actually have traveled.

Now I had supposed that I knew the roads of that state. I had driven them from end to end, side to side; I had driven them—or tried to—in every month out of the twelve. Three weeks before the news paper had proved that it was impossible to be mired on any of the main highways of the state I had been mired on a main highway of the state and had had to drive on low or intermediate for fifty straight miles.

From all of which we learn the moral that there are no bad roads in any state in the Union—not if you name the state. But until certain states which we will not under any conditions name—there are about forty of them—make their roads five hundred per cent better than they are now, neither cheap transportation of food nor long-distance touring will even begin. But there is coming a day when an average not-wealthy tourist will in a month's vacation see Boston and New Orleans, the Grand Cañon and San Francisco and the brown sea sands. And in that day we shall be more eager Americans, more understanding of our far-sundered neighbors.

Boost Highways Legislation

Already we have Federal aid for state roads, Congress is considering the Townsend Bill to create national highways linking all the large cities of the country; authorized road repairs delayed by the war have been resumed. But there is still something for the plain citizen to do. He can encourage his congressman to favor constant increase of Federal construction; his state assemblyman to vote for state extension of the Federal system; and particularly he can work for state and county bond issues. And he can join automobile associations and clubs—the most active and effective of forces advocating good roads legislation.

But properly marked and made roads may deprive you of asking directions, which is the soundest topic of touring conversation!

You stop at the corner of Third and Oak streets in front of the signboard advertising plug tobacco. You get out the map and demand of your wife: "Don't you think this road by way of Thompson's Forge looks kind of roundabout?" Of course she doesn't know anything more about it than you do, but it's comforting to have someone agree with you. While you are driving west on Main Street you explain why you don't stop and ask directions and then you stop and ask directions of the ancient old man leaning on the rural mail box under the big cottonwood tree.

"What's the best way to Midgeton?"

"Midgeton, eh? Going to Midgeton? Where ye come from?"

"Just driven in from Pearlapolis. What's the best —"

"Pearlapolis, eh? Well, ye come quite a ways. Now I'll tell ye. If I was going to Midgeton I wouldn't take the county road. I'd take the road that turns left at Pem Bemis'. Know where Pem's place is?"

"No, I've never been through here before."

"I see. Well, ye keep right on west here a ways, about three-four miles—no, I guess maybe it's six miles, say seven—and ye come to the schoolhouse—but mind ye, don't turn off at the first schoolhouse—now wait, this'll make it clearer. Know where the New Baden Creamery is?"

You Can't Miss It, Eh!

"No, I've never been through here before."

"Well, ye bear to the left and when ye come to the second schoolhouse on the left—not the one on the right—no, that's wrong; it's the one on the right—you turn to the right—no, I'm kind of balled up ye turn to the left and go northeast about two hundred rods, maybe five hundred, and turn to the right and Keep straight on into Midgeton. Ye can't miss it."

"Thank you."

You drive on out of his sight and stop and complainingly demand of the passenger: "Which was the first turn—to the right or the left?"

"Yes!"

No matter what the guide says he will unquestionably wind up with "You can't miss it."

I wish people wouldn't do that. I'll bet I can miss any road ever laid out. Once I missed the Lincoln Highway at noon on a clear day. Once I spent from nine P. M. to seven A. M. in driving from New York to Philadelphia, a distance of ninety miles if you go straight. It was night and foggy. We had aboard a man from Newark and he kept assuring us that with him as pilot we couldn't miss it, Newark having the strategic position of being near to all American cities except possibly Honolulu and New York.

We stopped happily in a populous street to ask if this was Elizabeth and found that it was Bayonne. Later we saw in the distance, beyond rivers and mounds of mist, a large city which was, I think, either Toronto or Ciudad Porfirio Diaz—we never knew, because when we tried to stalk it through the fog we lost it and have never been able to find it since.

Nineteen times that nebulous night we asked directions of people by the road, and every time the kind-hearted adviser wound up with "You can't miss it."

But it was rather sporting. Except for that gift of missing the way which every spirited autohobo possesses, we should never have been sitting in a smoke-clotted lunch room in a dark Jersey city when the night shift came out of the factories, nor have found that romance of light and shadow which in long-distance motoring—you can't miss it!

Part 2

Want a Lift

A globe trotter whom I know, a discouragingly prosperous person with an estate and a wrist watch and things like that, was driving me through Illinois. We were muddy and not too well manicured. We had left the car and were walking into town for an inner tube. A plump young man with tortoise-shell glasses, an expensive roadster and an expensive girl stopped us to ask road directions, and being obliging persons we got out a series of maps which looked like the filing cases in the kick-and-inquiry department of a mail-order house.

Yet as we went on we weren't boiling over with the fellowship of the road whereby all honest autohoboes become Pollyandrews.

For the girl had watched us, first with obvious fear that we would ask for a lift, then with that silken, cynical amusement which in novels is attributed to vampires but in real life fits no one but cafeteria cashiers. She had been so entertained by the thought of one who lived on Lake Shore Drive mingling with the poor and humble along the road. I am sure that as they drove away she said to her unfortunate husband, "Fancy! How quaint!"

We were. The globe-trotter informed me that I had a blob of mud on the end of my nose, which is no nose to be needlessly featured that way. Even so, the cynical lady was a historic example of how not to enjoy motor touring. For though scenery is all right in its place — which is never on the ends of noses, by the way — and though a handy liar can make more out of speed stories and miles per gallon than out of hints about his profits in oil, yet the liveliest pleasure of automobumming is picking up stray people and learning how curiously like millionaires and famous sculptors they are.

And when a fellow driver in an object like a startled Scotch terrier wants to stop on the road and gossip with you he is honoring you. Probably he has just hiked from Moose Jaw to Tia Juana.

The most engaging people I ever encountered in touring were three who came all in a row through Oregon and California. We had for that trip a flivver with the tonneau filled with baggage covered by an army blanket, which made a lumpy platform on which had roosted harvest hands and Chinks and district teachers.

The Long Road to the Poorhouse

Ahead on an Oregon mountain road we saw a thick-shouldered old man with long white hair painfully worming down the pike. His big flat feet scuffled through the dust, scarcely lifting; his steps could not have been more than three inches in length.

We stopped.

"Want a lift?"

He peered up with red-netted eyes, bewildered. Dirt was permanently embedded in his bristly gashed wrinkles. His hand shook. He wore an overcoat frayed in uncouth embroidery at the skirts. He carried a bundle in a red bandanna handkerchief and his staff was the steel rod of an old umbrella with a tarnished silveroid handle.

"What say?" he trembled.

"Want a lift?"

Timidly, "Oh! T'anks!"

"We had to help him up on the running board, to a seat on the kit in the tonneau. His bundle and his stick with the proud silver handle we tossed in front. He shrieked, "Oh, my cane! My clothes! Vot you done wit' em'?" He kept it up, terrified as a child, till we put them within reach of his hand.

"Where you bound for?" I asked over my shoulder as we went on.

"I'm going *bei* the poorhouse."

"Good Lord—uh—where's that?"

"In Blankburg, forty miles from here."

"And you were going to walk it?"

"*Ja*, sure. Vy not?"

"How many miles can you walk in a day?"

"Four. But yesterday I valk six! Yes, sir! And I'm eighty-seven years olt!"

This was just before the arrival of the word "cootie" had made it customary to discuss certain features of the gay, jocund, gypsying hobo, but I knew what my wife was thinking. And it was a nice, heavy, infestable blanket on which the old man was sitting. The more we reflected upon him the more we wished that somebody else had picked him up. But you do not drop a man who is taking ten days to walk to the poorhouse.

He was German, it seemed. He admitted that he "didn't talk English very gute." But then he had been in America only seventy-one years. For forty years he had been a California sheep herder. He had seen the world though—oh, sure.

"Vunce," he confided, "I vos valking in California and a fellow give me a ride and vot you t'ink? He vos a millionaire! Vy, dot fellow, he had a vatch chain as big arount as my little finger!"

I shrank in my seat; I tried to look modest behind the flivver steering wheel, which is awfully small to look modest behind. My own watch chain was as thin as a string. But some day I'm going to have a chain as big round as his thumb and I'm going to hang nine lodge emblems on it, so that people will know that I'm fashionable and wealthy—and I'm going back to Oregon and take that old man out riding again.

After his boast he looked us all over and said compassionately, "Dis ain't a very big auto, eh? Vell, dot's all right for folks like us. Vere you vork? You look a lot like a bartender I know. He used to vork on the section gang at Cocolalla, Idaho."

We slid through cañons, between tree-furred cliffs, and like a true tenderfoot I hopefully tried to impress the old man. I sped up. I did what seemed to me very neat things in the way of coasting. But that ancient sheep herder, rocking in a bored way on the back porch of the flivver, occasionally almost sliding off into the river below the road, yawned and dozed and wakened only to fumble and see if his bundle and his fine stick were safe.

One Garage for Every Forty Persons

We climbed; we slid down a mountain; the brakes promptly burned out; and through the dusk — the driver playing low and reverse as though they were organ pedals — we went careening down an exclamatory hill and popped unexpectedly into a town which the Lord created on Blue Monday. All we could see of it was a garage. But that to the autohobo is all there is to see. The garage is his railroad station, laundry, state capitol, ostrich farm, convention building and art gallery.

The garage man was still in his shop. He was sixty, his mustache was sandy and uncertain of direction — in fact, on the wrong road entirely. He spat between syllables.

Could he put in a brake band?

We-ul, his mechanic had just quit him, but guessed he could — seen it done 'nough times. Have the Liz ready for us by eight in the morning.

I decided that at least he knew more about it than I did. I was wrong. I knew more than he did. I knew nothing.

He said that there was a good hotel — for a town of the size. And what was the size? Oh, about forty! We started for it on foot.

The sheep herder trailed after us and wailed, "Vot you do'?"

"We're going to stay at the hotel."

"You say you take me *bei* the poorhouse!"

"We will to-morrow. To-night you can stay at the hotel."

"But—please, mister—I ain't—I only got five cents."

"That's all right. I'll pay for it."

"Me stay at a hotel? My, dot's fine! But it cost a lot—maybe more as two bits."

"That's all right:"

"Please, mister—please, could you gif me the money and I pay? I don't vant they should t'ink I vos a bum. Or please, could you maybe say I was your uncle? Dot's it. You tell 'em I'm your uncle."

The garage man was too trusting. It was not a good hotel for a town with as large a population as forty. We were shown by the proprietress to a room which, aside from lacking sheets, pillows, blankets, soap, towels and water—either running or firm—was fully furnished. The landlady wore men's shoes and she had a harelip. We pointed out to her that we'd love to have this and that added to the room. She looked about vaguely and admitted in slow astonishment that the hired girl must have forgotten something.

Could she attend to it? Oh, ye-es, she t-thought so; she'd have to see about it. This evening? Why, she'd try to—she sure would.

Into the room bounced the real manager of the hotel, the landlady's daughter, a sharp-nosed child of fifteen with more brains than the landlady and the garage man put together. In fact, she had practically normal mentality. She snapped: "You hustle down and finish getting supper, ma, and then make up a bed here. "Say, you"—to us—"your friend is wandering round hollering. I give him a nice two-bit room, but he won't stay in it. You better tend to him."

The poor old sheepman, it proved, could not see by lamplight. In his room he had fumbled about and found that his bundle and his fine silver-headed stick were missing; and these, after seventy-five years of drudgery, were all he had. Down in the filthy lower corridor we discovered him inching his way along with his fingers against the wall and crying in his darkness, "My clothes! Dey took my clothes!"

We restored his baggage, which had been left in the office. He held it to his breast, stroked his stick — the rod of an umbrella! He would not leave them again. He took them in to supper and guarded them in his lap.

Supper was an acrobatic exhibition. There was one long table, mostly occupied by men in shirt sleeves, who humped over and flapped their elbows and chawed and said nothing. The food consisted of coffee — curse the man who invented adulterants for good tasty cowpeas — with soda-caked bread, beef stew, and flapjacks made of fresh library paste. We went away from supper rather speedily. Were there, we inquired, ever any movies? Well, the landlady cheered us, there had been a missionary lecture with colored slides only about three months ago.

What's a Nut or Two in the Magneto!

The new brake band was not quite ready at eight next morning, but at ten the garage man glowingly announced that the car was "all O. K." Our sheep herder had not appeared. We were cowards and poltroons — I had never till then known what a poltroon was, but I saw that I was it. We paid the garage man two dollars to drive the herder to the poorhouse when he should rise and we hastily prepared to sneak out of town.

As I started the flivver — all the machine guns of the Western Front went off at once just beneath my feet. That, the garage man insisted, was all right. Maybe he had dropped a nut into the magneto while putting in the band.

Yes, maybe he had dropped in a nut — and maybe he had dropped in four or five nuts, and maybe he had dropped in his pliers, his jack, the forge and one or two crowbars. In fact, if he ever misses anything from his garage I'll give him the address of the man to whom I sold the flivver in San Francisco after the magneto had gone bankrupt.

We nervously ventured on all day, fondly hating to leave each safe garage that we passed — and sometimes being so overwhelmed by our love for them that we didn't pass, but stopped and let the garage man tell us that he would like to perform a laparotomy on the magneto. We took the magnificent road over the Siskiyous into California and came down into the sunset. The next afternoon in a gully between two viciously steep hills, fourteen miles or so from any garage, we stopped for keeps. I poked round with the large screw driver, the small screw driver and the wrench I had stolen from my brother. I tightened the spark plugs and looked wise and told my wife what the trouble was. But at the same time I should have liked to know what the trouble was.

The car was blocking the narrow way. Up behind it rattled an astounding vehicle—a flivver with a delivery body filled with trunks and cooking pots and a big roll of canvas. Its occupants were an unshaven man in greasy overalls and a plump comfortable wife in a raincoat.

Ah, here was a workman, maybe a garage man! Here was that beautiful fellowship of the road and come-comrade-vagabonds-let-us-roam-the-jolly-old-world-together stuff. Here were those humble sterling virtues that renew one's faith. He wasn't a gentleman autohobo; in fact, he looked as though he knew something. I shot a few palpitant smiles in his direction and waited his assistance.

He hurtled out, ran to me, clamored, "What the hell you stopping up the way for?" In much dignity, not very well concealing the fact that I wished to hit him with the rear axle, I stated, "I should be very glad to get out of your way if you care to help me push the car off the road. So sorry that a little thing like a complete breakdown has delayed your important mission."

You know—haughty and reproving.

"Grrrrrr! You amateur sagebrush tourists give me a big fat pain. Don't know enough to get your Liz out of the garage."

"Say, you can go plumb —"

"Grrrrrr! Get out of the way!"

He pushed me aside, steadily cursing; he looked at the transmission cover and asked a few impertinent questions and wailed that he should once more have been afflicted by one of these goats that infest the road and spoil driving for a real guy; he held up his hands in agony and informed heaven that he'd be danged if he'd be fool enough to help anybody again or even give 'em any information; and then he told me that my "fool mag was shorted," and he worked on the car for one hour and a quarter and made the repairs, and when I tried to pay him at the end he viewed me with great distaste and roared:

"Go on! If you paid me what it was worth you wouldn't have enough money left to get to Frisco. Get out of here! Don't go on blocking up the road! Drive on, will yuh?"

"S-say, I'm-I'm awfully obliged—w-wish you'd let me pay you, but—I'll drive off the road and you go on ahead."

"Naw! Gwan ahead! Man like you hadn't ought to be let out on the highway. Not one of these damn amateurs that know anything. Stopping up the road! Gwan ahead—you'll probably bust down again in ten miles and if I'm not behind you most anything will happen to you and ought to!"

Furiously he returned to his car and his wife said placidly, "My, how you do curse and swear!"

Twice more that day he rescued us. Each time he refused to go on ahead.

Meeting Messrs. Ig and Nition

At nightfall there was only one mountain between us and a sizable town at which we planned to spend the night. We climbed blissfully, we reached a plateau and we halted with abruptness. The magneto was tired and desired to go by-by. There was no chance of our friend's coming—he had said that he would stop and make camp before dusk. It was a rocky, scraggly, uninhabited stretch of mountain. There was no garage, no telephone for miles.

Another flivver hopped into sight, but the two men in it knew less about ignition than I did—they knew less about it than any other person in the world except the garage man who had salted my magneto with hardware. They did, however, help me to get my car off the single-track road. It was a job. One side of the road was a well-ventilated nothing-at-all, with an excessively airy drop to boulders two hundred feet below. We had to push the car down to a slight widening, checking it all the way with stones under the wheels, get it off the road and let it rest with the back against a pine tree on the edge of the cañon.

While we were working, strangers tugging as hard as though this were their own wreck, a big car with eight cylinders and much upholstery passed by. The driver looked bored, but the woman beside him was more than bored; her contemptuous stare showed resentment at having to witness three greasy men working over a cheap automobile. That was three years ago and the woman took less than three seconds in passing; but I have not forgotten her glance or ceased to be sorry for her. I have no doubt that she is doing well socially. They probably let her in at some of the dances at the Sacramento Country Club or the San Jose Golf Association. But it must hurt her so to have to go on living among common people.

When the car was safe my wife and I prepared to camp — and interestedly discovered that we hadn't much of anything with which to camp. We had intended to stay at hotels; we had let the larder dwindle to a can of corned-beef hash, a few spoonfuls of coffee and a glass of raspberry jam.

I shall always be doubtful about faith healing. Maybe it can cause a man with acute peritonitis to run seven miles and eat a fried pork chop, but it failed with us. We sat up on a mountain and told each other that there would be a lot of landscape if it weren't dark and that raspberry jam certainly did take the place of both sugar and cream in coffee. The jam resisted our faith cure. It continued to make the coffee taste like the shaving cream when you get it on the brush instead of tooth paste.

We poured out the coffee and spoke well of corned-beef hash washed down with pure, wholesome cold water.

That mountain side was covered with sharp flints and we were too tired to pitch our tent; but we made beds with the pneumatic mattress for the passenger and the two seat cushions for myself. They were comfortable, and after an hour of exhilarating worry as to whether we should ever get off that mountain before I grew a beard and a taste for moonshining, I was dropping asleep—when I thought of bears.

It was my first mountain camp. Hadn't I read things about bears here? Of course all Americans are heroic. Look at the A. E. F. I wasn't afraid of a grizzly—two grizzlies. But I didn't want to hurt them. Wasn't there something about the Government protecting these brothers of the wild? How thoughtless and inconsiderate of me it would be to go to Leavenworth for kicking a seven-foot grizzly on his tender nose. I solemnly wavered through the darkness to the car and brought back my single-barrel shotgun. It was a gun capable of stopping the charge of the largest and most ferocious tadpole. My wife inquired what I intended to do with it. I did not explain. In three years now I have never yet thought up a really good, conclusive, masculine answer.

There was a fog in the morning, and we looked at the remains of corned-beef hash and coffee au gratin and wished the bears had got us. The car—there is something impressively permanent and absolute about a broken-down car. It sits there with its foolish back up against a pine tree and it hasn't yielded and fixed itself even yet.

We humped up in the Arcadian nook and waited for passers-by. Down the road was a clatter, a rattle—then two revolver shots. It was the surly man who had repaired my magneto. He was waving his pistol. He came up grinning, with "I had a hunch you poor hams would be stuck again. Had any breakfast?"

"No!"

"We thought we'd wait for ours till we caught up with you. Ma, shake up a little breakfast, can you?"

While he worked over the magneto, his plump, placid wife prepared bacon and eggs and real coffee with condensed milk and real sugar; and she chuckled at us and told us we looked like a couple of plush sofas that had been left out in the rain.

All day we trailed on ahead of them, descending from the mountains, plodding through the glaring Sacramento, Valley, with the Sierra Nevadas on one side and the Coast Range a filminess on the other. At night we watched them make camp in a town park, where a dozen other friendly cars were noisy with laughter and banjos.

Philosophers of the Highway

The man constructed a comfortable and weather-tight house in six minutes by opening the folded ridgepole, thrusting two uprights into standards fore and aft, pitching a canvas tent over the whole car and spreading the good thick mattress on the floor. His wife insisted on giving us dinner. We wanted them to dine with us at the hotel, but they refused.

"Nope, I'm not shaved. Fact, I think I'll harvest the crop right now."

When he had finished I realized that he was a handsome man. His thin face and high forehead and hooked nose had the edged fineness of William Gillette — or Sherlock Holmes.

He told his story, and I found that here of all the world were two people who had solved the problem of happiness. Though they were under fifty they had done their work.

They had brought up children, who were married and independent. They had saved enough money for a stake in old age. Now they were seeing the world. He was an expert angle-iron smith. Sometimes he worked in the naval shops at Bremerton and Mare Island; sometimes in motor service stations anywhere from Yreka to Denver. His wages were seven to ten dollars a day and he saved more than half. Whenever he became restless, said his wife, "Pa comes home and grins at me and he says, 'Ma, let's throw the skillet in, the Lizzie and go some place,' and we start next morning and hike round for three months."

With a special carburotor they used distillate for fuel at half the cost of gasoline. They always camped out and the blacksmith did his own repairing. They could travel a thousand miles on twenty dollars, and when they stayed for a month in a mountain pass and the smith went hunting the month cost them two dollars for salt pork and coffee and sugar. They had the wanderlust and they satisfied it. They had beaten the game of civilization. They were supreme philosophers and people in high-powered cars passed them by, unseeing.

Of course his employers must have resented his leaving on a day's notice, but before he began his roving he had had thirty or more years of steady and expert toiling; he had by even the strictest philosophy of industry earned the right to be irregular. And all up and down the coast there must be some thousand or two motorists who bless the fact that now and then he stops, curses them, tells them that he cannot abide the sight of their ignorance and then saves their lives.

Not that they bless to any advantage of course. He told me that out of the hundreds whom he had helped and who had fervently asked for his permanent address, not one had ever written to him, not one of those over whose cars he had worked for hours had ever sent him so much as a post card.

The last we saw of the blacksmith and his wife was under a bridge ten miles from Sacramento. As we rattled upon the bridge there was a horrible scream, a revolver shot. We pulled up with a jar, and there in the dusk was the blacksmith. He had bought a steak and his wife and he were waiting for us. They had waited two hours.

I have found that this southern hospitality does exist; I have had a broker show me what his favorite New York hotel can do; but I never have found, and never from Port Said to Copenhagen shall I find, a gayer graciousness than that of the blacksmith whom we met along the road.

Guide-book information about the route is just a little deader than free silver and hieroglyphs. The one way to taste and feel the country is to coax wayfarers to have a lift and ask them questions.

Once I even received some philological information which I shall be proud to let the American Etymological

Association have if they will give me a degree. A harvester whom we picked up in the gray lava folds of Moses Coulee in Washington explained the name.

"They call this here place a coulee, because it's cooler in summer — why, I thought everybody knew that!"

The most picturesque and most doubtful person to transport is the long-distance automobile-lift hobo. He is a new species of vagrant. He wears reasonably good clothes, he speaks admirable English, he is well shaved and cleanhanded and he makes a business of permitting autohoboes to enjoy feeling charitable. He hikes merrily along the way until a motorist picks him up and instead of forty miles of St. Vitus dance on a freight-car brake beam in a typhoon of dust and cinders he delicately indulges in a hundred-mile spin. He becomes particular about his stable and he will sniffily refuse to ride in a humble, useful vehicle which resembles a recently batted cockroach. He prefers a limousine and if he goes far enough in his profession he is particular about the upholstery and his host's cigars. He is refreshing and a proof that the meek may inherit the earth, but the gally ones are the executors of the estate.

If the automobile-lift bum is lucky he meets a man driving alone. Driving alone for long distances is the most desolate of sports. Your thoughts go round and round in tedious circles; you mumble, "Let's see — now let me see. Ought to have 'em look at that spring. Squeaking — yump. Ought to — ought to do that. Must remember that." And at night you are outside of the world, shut off by darkness from all friendliness forever. You drive on, dour, dumb, cramped, hypnotized by the sliding road.

The solitary is glad to tote the agreeable hobo and even to buy his meals. Why not? The tramp sings excellently for his supper; he is better company than most respectable cits; a traveling companion is not to be chosen for his soundness in judging clothes-pin timber. At the same time, if an automobile-lift bum tells you about that charming couple from New York who have recently taken him two thousand miles and put him up at the best hotels you needn't believe him. He is not giving you information. He is giving you an invitation to enter the charity contest. I am sending my secretary and the office detective to trail that generous couple. I have heard about them from seven different hoboes now. The last time was from the Irish poet whom we picked up in Tennessee.

The Unridden Guest

He was a bright-eyed, quick-glancing, sleek-haired young man, and we were cheerful in our hail. He was in the tonneau before we had reached the "f" in lift. He needed no coaxing to enter into diverting conversation. He leaned forward with his hands on the back of the front seat and I could feel his superior smile boring the back of my neck.

"How far you going?" I asked. "Clear into Bristol?"

"Oh, yes, I go to Bristol. How far you going?"

"Why, uh, why—" I had the hunch that it was risky to tell him. We were tacitly struggling. He wanted to tie me up with a contract. He thrust hard.

"Going clear through?"

"Why—why, yes, in a way. How far you going?"

"To Washington, D. C."

"Oh!" I meant "Ouch."

He was a nice young man, but I felt that he would help us out too much in our conversation. I was wishing that I could courteously unlift the lift. He was offering, "I'll be glad to stick by you as far as you want. I've tramped all the way from New Orleans—except where I got rides. Most folks like to have me along. I'm a pretty good driver and mechanic. I'm always glad to help people out. I met one couple from New York. They were awfully nice people—rich too. They took me three hundred miles. They were nice people."

I wanted to be nice people, too, but—

"Oh, yes," I said.

"Going as far as Washington?"

"Why, kind of a different way."

"Where to?"

He was so authoritative this time that I feebly admitted, "To Philadelphia."

"Oh, well, I suppose I could go to Washington that way."

I peeped back. He was examining me with scorn. His talents had been wasted on me.

"Most people don't appreciate motor touring," he announced.

"No?"

"No—they—do—not! They haven't got any savvy—any—any romance. They can't let themselves go and be vagrants. They are so wrapped up in their fool business cares—what do you do for a living?"

"I am the treasurer of the Lilywhite Noodle Company," I asserted. I am sorry to have to record that the vagrant had no trouble in believing me. He groaned: "Oh, Lawerd! Well, I suppose—personally, all I know about the habits of noodles is that they aren't becoming to whiskers." He laughed quite a little at his original humor.

"Now me, I'm a poet!"

"Really?"

"Sure am! And I've had some stories published."

"It must be great to be an author. Where were they published?"

"I had one in a Houston newspaper and others—you know—different places."

"Just how can a fellow sit down and write all this stuff?" I marveled.

Spies on Point Thisanthat

"It's perfectly easy—if you have the temperament. Now you, I suppose you see things in terms of noodles! Not that I blame you. I don't suppose you can help it. When you see a mountain you probably think of a pile of dough, and I suppose a pretty girl must mean another sale of macaroni! But a poet—well, I wander round—"

"In my car!" I grumbled to myself.

"—and have wonderful thoughts and make notes. Here's a note I made to-day. 'The sky is like a sapphire.' Can you get that? Think of it—like a jewel! Let me tell you, I always feel a fellow ought to pass on some of his gift. When you're on a trip like this, why can't you forget your darn business and let Nature inspire you? Of course I wouldn't want to intrude, but I do believe I could teach you and your good lady to forget the factory and the babies and all that rot. If you cared to have me, I'd be willing to go as far as Philadelphia and show you how a writer looks at things."

He liked the idea. Breathing warmly upon our necks, the rapidly less beloved vagabond instructed us:

"Do you see that hill over there? It's like feathers of an Orient bird."

It did resemble feathers. It was like a six-year-old boa after the baby had played choo-choo cars with it. But I could not concentrate upon it. I was afraid that I was going to be instructed for the next five days, clear into Philadelphia.

"Another thing: I don't believe you keep the carbon cleaned out of your car. I'm kind of an expert on motors. I'll be glad to help you —"

My wife turned half round. She looked at the poet with feminine inappreciation. She said in a high clear voice: "I am so sorry, but we can take you only to Bristol. Now if you don't mind—if you will pardon us—we were discussing a new recipe for our noodles."

I hope the poet never tries to manufacture noodles by the recipe which we worked out. As I remember it, I suggested making the wrappers out of turnip skins. Chefs have since assured me that comparatively few noodles have wrappers. It makes the overhead so large.

When we dropped the poet in Bristol he condescended: "You folks have been very kind. I hope you won't mind my writing a story about you. I always get types at the first glance. There's something so droll in the thought of a noodle manufacturer and his good wife getting out into the open and risking the peril and madness of beauty! Good-by."

He must have been a poet, too, the man whom we

overhauled in the Montana sagebrush twenty miles from anywhere. At our invitation he shook his head.

"Nope, I guess I'll just peg along."

"But it looks like a long hike."

"I suppose so. But if you were to take me five hundred miles I wouldn't be any nearer to where I'm going. I'm not going anywheres. I'm just going."

My friend the war correspondent was also refused the favor of giving a lift. Driving through New Hampshire he stopped pityingly when he saw a woman beginning the climb of a mile-long upgrade. The correspondent is considerably under forty and the woman was considerably over sixty, sallow and squirrel-toothed and spinsterine.

He raised his hat and begged: "May I give you a ride, madam?"

She glared. She snapped: "No, sir, you can't! I don't do that sort of thing!"

It was the correspondent and I who were driving through Massachusetts in 1918 and saw a uniformed Y. M. C. A. man having difficulties with his car. We asked if we could help. He strolled up to us and chirped, "Motoring? So am I. Great sport."

"Doing Y work near here?" asked the correspondent.

"I'm not really with the Y. That's my disguise, I'm a secret-service man," he gloated.

"That must be very interesting."

"Oh, it is." He delightedly put his foot up on the running board, rested his arm on his knee and launched out:

"We suspect there's some German spies on the coast and my organization chose me to run them down. Last night I almost caught one."

"No! Go on! Really?"

"I did! His name is Blankenfritz and he's got a place out on Point Thisanthat. There's an abandoned lighthouse on it and he's mounted a big searchlight and I figured out that he was signaling submarines. I hung round there all last night, but he kept mum. But he can't escape me. And I'm watching for another fellow who's disguised as a peddler. Doesn't know anybody is on his trail, so don't speak about it. Well, I guess I'll get back to work. Just pumping up a tire. Good —"

"Wait! Wait! Are you a regular member of the secret service—do you belong to the M. I. D., or what?"

"Naw. Those fellows are too tied up with red tape. Maybe I'll accept a commission in the M. I. D. to help 'em out, but I represent a private league of prominent citizens. Well, so long."

It's awful to think of the risks a spy runs, with bloodhounds like that on his trail all the time.

My wife and I were in the Northern Minnesota pines when we found the lost dreamer. On a one-way trail through the gray trunks we drove into a clearing and discovered an abandoned lumbering town. Here fifteen years ago a hulking slab-fed sawmill had shot flame through its screened chimney; and the forty stores and saloons of Main Street were jammed with roaring lumberjacks, Maine Yank and Nova Scotian, Swede and Finn and pea-soup Canuck, in fur caps and clumping corks and checkerboard shirts and mackinaws of orange and blue and russet. Now there was only the sound of desertion and the tapping needles of yellowed Norway pines round an enormous pile of bleached sawdust, a tiny shack of a planing mill and one lone gaunt store building with the sign "Board'g House."

I hustled up to the boarding house—but the hustle seemed foolish in that stilled ruin. I had been sure I wanted water for the radiator, but did it matter—did anything matter? I yawned up to the door. I would probably find a grouchy old hermit or no one at all. No matter.

Through the screenless screen door peered a man with white fine hair, thin white mustache, pink soft cheeks, anxious eyes that had once seen many things, eyes of a man who might have been a diplomat and a wanderer to strange ports.

"May I go round to your pump and get a little water for the car?"

"Ye-es."

When I reached the pump he was already filling a lard

pail for me. He hesitated; then: "I noticed there was a lady in your car. Wouldn't she like a little hot tea, maybe?

"Oh, no, we don't want to bother—"

Then I understood. He was disappointed. He was lonely and wanted to talk. "Sure, we would like some. We were going to lunch on some sandwiches."

"Won't you bring them in?"

We did. He spread newspapers on a long oilcloth-covered table in what had been the front room of the store and was now a living room choked with bare benches and a paunchy stove and lined with blurred Halftones from Sunday papers. He hastened to make mugs of tea, with condensed milk.

"It's pretty quiet here," we suggested.

"Yes, it is: There's just three men left here, working in the shingle mill, using up some old bolts. I keep house for them. I"— he looked at us timidly—"I haven't always been a cookee. I used to be a printer. I could set more ems an hour than any other man in the chapel."

"You were? I'm a newspaper man."

He choked: "This is the first time in more than five years that I've met anyone that knew what I was talking about! I've been—I tried to start a little store on a reservation, but it failed; and I was bull cook in a lumber camp and—I guess I'm too old to do much and I'll always have to stick here now. The boys here—they're nice fellows, but they're Polacks and don't talk English much and they go to sleep pretty early and I guess they don't care much about print shops. My fingers are all thumbs from the rheumatism and I can't stick type any more. I wish—oh, well, the owner treats me fine."

I assured him that I could still find at least the "e" box in the lower case and keep out of the way of type lice, and the old man fluttered with agitation. He asked of the new ways in publishing. Had I ever seen the office of a New York paper? Had I really seen Irvin Cobb and Will Irwin and Frederick Palmer and Sam Blythe and James Hopper?

His beautiful old head lifted; his diffident hope that

we would like him turned into the easy friendliness of the man who has once been popular; we could see him, with the greasy kitchen apron gone, wearing the green eye shade that was the sign of his craft, setting the story of a war, a flood, a big fight, or secretly correcting the tenses of a cub who was "a regular fellow, but weak on grammar."

And where had he worked, what had he done? — we hinted.

Oh, nothing much. Just stuck type. Well, there had been times — with the help of faith and a cross-eyed mule he had lugged a Washington hand press and a hatful of type up a mountain ridge and started the first newspaper in a town. Otherwise composed of prospectors, salt pork and booze. He had elected a congressman and chased a would-be horsewhipper seven blocks. Later he had lived through a Michigan forest fire, and — only one day late in going to press — had brought the paper out on butcher's paper.

Waylaying a Ranchman

It was time for us to get on if we were to make the Iron Range. He tried to hold us; he cunningly tried to lead us into politics and religion; he showed us his little treasures, his Indian curios and the wonderful jackknife his grandnephew had sent him. But we were due at the house of a friend.

As we started the car he begged, "Wait a moment!"

He ran into the house and came back with one lone, tattered magazine, beseeching, "Maybe your lady would like to read this to-night."

I had seen the magazine among his traps. This old man, the lover of books, had brought us in farewell his whole library — the only thing in the world he had to read.

Once it was we who served tea, and we served it to a ranchman in the Bad Lands of North Dakota. Cow-puncher movies rarely show Hard Boiled Harry drinking tea and eating lady fingers on a butte, but can do.

As we drove out of Medora, where Roosevelt went to town in his ranching days, I spotted a long-mustached man, his wise old eyes puckered with wind and dust, his boots stitched into a leather rose garden, loping out on his pony.

"How can we pick him up?" I speculated.

"Let's waylay him. Let's be having tea when he comes along. If he thinks we're Anglomaniacs and wants to shoot us we'll tell him we're English."

We got out a box of extremely dry lady fingers, which we carried because they do stand transportation—and because lady fingers are so much like blotting paper in taste and use that they remind a writer of home. We boiled water on a solid-alcohol stovelet.

When the old ranchman came along and glanced at us, on a rock above the road, we hailed, "Hungry? Light and set!"

That was dialect. It may have been Western dialect or Southern dialect or Jewish dialect, or maybe it wasn't any special kind, but just dialect.

He rode straight up the face of the rock, and in delight at having these particularly tender tenderfeet to impress, the pony reared and came down safely between the tea and the dainty, vanilla-flavored blotters.

"There was an English lord that used to have tea every afternoon back in the hills. He was the one that stole my store pants and married the Sioux squaw," the ranchman said mildly.

"Did that prejudice you permanently? Won't, you have some tea to make up for the pants?" begged my wife.

"Lady, my old dad, down in Missoura, he taught me that this unpardonable sin that the elder used to preach about was refusing vittles when you're offered 'em."

He told us of old-time mule skinners and bad men who to this day live back in the folds and gullies of the Bad Lands; of the Marquis De Mores, who founded Medora, dreaming of a grand duchy for himself, and in the early '80's in this land of rattlers and buttes and unquenchably burning lignite and handy six-guns erected a château.

After tea we drove on for two miles. Then on a slope the car went gently to sleep. Probably it desired to dream of marquises. Or the fact that we were down to one gallon of gas may have had something to do with it.

Our friend, the rancher, came in sight again. He shook his head, worried.

"This is the last steep climb before you get out on the prairie. If I can get you up it you'll be all right. If I can't I'll take you over to my shack for the night."

He insisted on hitching the car to his little pony and trying to tow us. Not a budge. He sat miserable.

A flivver larruped into sight. The rancher swung off his hat and gravely addressed the driver:

"Could you lend these folks some gasoline? They're friends of mine and—I don't know what's the matter with me. They've been awful good to me and here I've gone and laid down on them."

We got the gasoline.

I don't know, but I'm afraid there is a moral somewhere in the tale, and a hint about what the motorist discovers regarding human nature, once he gets away from traffic cops and famous boulevards. It's pretty hard for an autohobo to go on being clever and cynical about people along the way.

Excuse Our Dust

As diverting as the people whom you pass are the intermittent—but sometimes not sufficiently intermittent—cars that are following the same trail; the car that is twice as big as yours, but that you triumphantly pass; and the confounded little squeaker that you ought to have left on the back track, but that persists in being just behind you.

There was an ancient and inescapable Lizzie which followed us from Wilmington to Baltimore the other day. It had no right to make more than ten miles an hour. But every time I stopped to look at a sign it went past me and the driver waved his hand in what he regarded as friendliness. Now no sensible driver cares who goes past him. Let 'em go if they want to. Decent autohoboes take time to look at the country. They plug on at a slow, reasonable rate. But—well, he shouldn't have waved his hand so insultingly. So I spent most of the trip in trying to show the poor idiot what a real car could do.

We lost him in Baltimore. Of course we did not gloat, but it was a satisfaction to know that he had learned his place. We didn't even look back to see if he continued lost — not more than twenty or thirty times between Baltimore and Washington, we didn't.

We serenely sailed into Washington, monarchs of the road. We stopped to look at a street sign. It was then that the road cootie skittered past us. He waved lovingly, and we followed him into the city — till he lost us.

I am glad that you, who drive sensibly, never do anything like that. I agree with you. What possible difference can it make if some duffer persists in thinking that you aren't the best amateur driver in America? In cases like that you show a proud humility as he goes by. And when you do step on her and almost shoot off the curve it isn't because you are irritated or jealous. It's just as you tell your alarmed and protesting wife:

"Rats! I'm not trying to get ahead of the poor nut. I merely want to see if the new piston rings are developing the power they ought to, considering — there, now I guess he'll stay back where he belongs! Let him eat my dust for a change!"

Some place in Idaho there is a man who if he knew where I was would come East and have a private mob and riot. He was one of these people seen intermittently on the same trail.

Our cars were parked side by side in a corral in Yellowstone Park, and in the evening when we were tuning up for the next day's drive he borrowed my hand pump. It is pleasant to lend things — it makes you understand what a high-minded, generous, beautiful character you are. In the bliss of that superiority I borrowed his electric hand torch — and immediately short-circuited it. The man said it didn't matter. He almost looked as though it didn't matter.

Next morning we were still friendly as we got out our

cars. We admitted that we were great drivers and that our cars were the only decent ones in the corral. I borrowed his hammer to swat a spring clip and the hammer came off. So did his smile.

He took the hammer away from me and said, "I'll fix it myself."

There is no gratitude in the world. Here I'd gone and lent an invaluable pump to this person and he'd already forgotten all about it.

I skipped out on the road and just in front of a twenty-per-cent grade my ignition quit.

My friend came up, scowled, and said patiently, "Oh, I suppose I'll have to haul you up."

He did—twice. He also broke his towrope. I thought he left me without any extreme amount of sadness. I don't believe he was brought up pious. Sometimes I don't believe he cared much if we never did meet again.

When I had finally crawled out of the park, with two cylinders and a sandwich missing, I hurried into the first garage. It was dark inside. I could barely see a car that was ahead of me. I yanked at the emergency brake, but I stopped with my front fenders nosing the tail of the other car. Out of it leaped a man who seemed displeased.

He bellowed, "You poor hunk of cheese, can't you see where you're going? Look at what you done to my fenders!"

It was my friend of the hand torch, the hammer, the hauls and the broken towrope. He saw who I was, but even so he didn't take that back—about the hunk of cheese. He groaned. He looked to heaven for comfort, but apparently didn't find any.

He wailed, "And I deliberately went and spoke to it first last night!"

He crawled back into his seat, mute. I didn't ask him what he meant. There are people with whom there's no use arguing.

I got into Livingston and stored my car late at night. Behind me was another car. The night attendant shouted

at its driver, "Nope, no room, Billy. This fellow gets the last inch of space."

"What'll I do?" lamented the outcast.

"How do I know? Go try the other garages, I suppose."

The discouraged driver peered from behind the windshield and saw me—saw who it was had the last inch. I wish to conceal who he was. But I will say that he studied me a little and muttered, "And if I'd stayed home the worst I'd have met would have been the jailer or the hangman."

He didn't look at me again. He sheltered his eyes and drove away.

The autohobo in a town of which he has never heard, which he casually finds on his route, makes friends who endure for years. Once in a pine forest we discovered a doctor and his wife, both of them under thirty, who had created a sanitarium with trained nurses and a modern equipment, and they lent us the hardest thing to get on a tour—a real bath ! Once among the buttes we brazenly picked up the commanding officer of an army post and his wife and an old-timer who had guided General Miles, and went rattlesnake hunting with them and to their delight and our carefully concealed anxiety—even found the snakes. And once in a Kentucky hill town we met Judge Priest, the real Judge Priest or his cousin, and in the basement court room at nine in the evening, with rows of chocolate faces banked at the windows, we heard him pass judgment on a darky who had gone wooing with a razor.

Caravansary Redivivus

They were and they remain our neighbors. To the real motor fanatic the only requirement for neighbors is that they live not more than ten miles from a passable road. The fact that they are also a thousand miles from his home is only incidental. The autohobo, a little weary of one street and one drug store and one movie theater, enlarges his neighborhood till the people he loves and daily remembers, are scattered from Spokane to Jacksonville; and the street he lives on is all of three thousand miles long—and ends at the Inn of Romance.

In the days of Harun-al-Rashid and the lure of Bagdad, the caravansary with its host of camels and its golden bales, its strangers black and white and brown in fez or turban or morion, was the hive of romance, the birthplace of thrilling tales; and still to-day at a Broadway theater we see enacted stories first devised by a fire of dung in the Syrian hills. The caravan has come again in the procession of motors with licenses from Massachusetts and Kansas, Florida and Utah, which all summer long fills the roads from coast to coast; and the caravansary is found again in dingy village inns.

Tellers of tales by the firelight we found in a little Montana town, and we forgot all the bad hotels and hard drives we had ever encountered. The proprietor had for years managed a factory in New York, but he had always, wanted the West and the hunting. At fifty-five he had bought this village hostelry. The usual barren office he had replaced by a livable room with a big fireplace; the usual hash he had apotheosized into flaky meat pies; and—only traveling men and autohoboes know what this means—he actually had running water in the bedrooms!

There was mud to the east and west after an unseasonable rain. All day long the veteran transcontinental drivers had been slogging on at eight miles an hour, getting oozily stuck every time they turned out to let a car pass. The oasis of the tiny hotel was filled with twenty motorists from ten states. At supper a Michigan professor sat beside a Portland banker who proudly asserted, "There's still good Oregon air in my tires."

Like all wanderers since Ulysses, we sat by the fire and forgot the mud and told lies. We boasted how fast we could travel and how few blow-outs we had and how we invariably "put it all over these fresh traffic cops."

A few days ago, in office or shop or study, each of us had been reasonably prosaic and standardized and modern and dull. We had turned into soldiers of fortune gathered at a tavern of the Low Countries in the days of Marco Polo, courteously believing the good stout lies, marveling at tales of far countries where there were giants with seven heads and all the maidens were rose and ivory. It was that fellowship which seemed to vanish forever when trains came in and passengers, unwillingly crowded in the long, narrow, swaying room, sat silent and suspicious till the journey's end or talked only of safe, vague, heavy things in pompous banalities. Not merely to Montana had the autohoboes driven, but to chivalry rediscovered—for Sir Philip Sidney sat with Baron Munchausen in front of the fire.

The fellowship of the road is not a sentimental fancy, but a reality. Only once have I found a thoroughly surly fellow motorist, one who refused a favor without reason. To make up for him there have been hundreds—

In back-country Virginia, in a wallow of yellow mud, my steering rod came unscrewed. A truck splashed up with two youngsters in overalls. I asked them to help me. They climbed out silently. And they worked with me for half an hour in the mud.

I cleared my throat in that foolish, indeterminate way males have when they are on unfamiliar ground and begged, "Now I want to pay you fellows —"

One of them looked at me, shook his head and stolidly plodded back to the truck. The other demanded, "Pay? For what? I reckon you'd have done the same thing for us. If drivers didn't help each other there wouldn't be much hope for the world. Seems like a fellow gets kind of shook out of himself when he gets out on the road. So long!"

Part 3

Part 3

The Great American Frying Pan

This is a howl, a protest, a kick and a letter to the papers. This is, as the thesaurus so daintily puts it, a suspiration, a flood of tears, a lachrymation, a coronach, a nenia, a jeremiad and an ullalulla. Particularly it's an ullalulla — a good strong ullalulla.

The author speaks as an authority on merchandising, being a member of that most important class of commercial authorities — the people who pay the bills. He has been elected to honorary membership in the Affiliated Sodality of Henry Dubbs. And he wished to record experiences with dealers on real Main Streets during several years of autohoboing.

His battle cry and the subject of his splendid and pervading grouch is the need of courtesy to customers and of artistic kicking by customers. It is a matter of importance. It makes much of the difference between a life that is interesting and a life that is a merely irritable scrabbling for bread. The reason why stories of gentlemen crooks are so popular is that unconsciously most people would rather be held up by a charming yegg than be given a job by a crank.

It would seem that after some millions of articles on the beauties of courtesy everybody must have been converted. But standing here before you and fearlessly facing this issue, my fellow citizens, we assert — and even ullalullate — that a large percentage of dealers haven't to this day heard of the bulletin that molasses is catching more flies than vinegar. At their present speed they will not hear of it till 2500 A.D.

Most of the celebrated reading public, when they skim over a persuasive sermon on courtesy, reflect, "That's an awfully good pointer for Bill Jones in the next block," and happily closing the magazine they glare at the low intruder who wants to interrupt their meditations by giving them money. No bad-tempered man over forty can without a private miracle see himself as bad tempered. If he understood that he — not his clerks or his bosses or his brother-in-law — wasn't invariably amiable the bank would in the next year see a doubling of his account.

A Subsolar Novelty—Courtesy

Every person in business has agreed to an unwritten contract not merely to perform his services honestly but also agreeably. The man who sells soap is not efficient if he so infuriates customers that they give up bathing. The man who snarls "I'm running this business to suit myself" isn't, as he thinks, either a hero, an independent thinker or an original wit. He is a criminal. When he hangs out his sign and thus invites the public in he is — whether he knows it or not — implying that he will give to everyone who enters as complete service as he can. And when he fails to do it he is not merely ill-advised; he is as disloyal, as dishonorable, as a soldier who deserts.

It would seem that all this must be common knowledge and practice; that any disquisition on courtesy to-day must be not only banal and humorless, but also ludicrously out of date.

But the author wishes by a few examples from some thousands of encounters with business men in thirty-three states during the past four years to indicate that far from being platitudinous to many merchants the idea of courtesy is only too startlingly new. And he suggests for this spiritual illness a spiritual remedy — the art of the efficient kick.

Most people spend most of their time in one place. They become used to Old Hank and dear, bluff, blustering old Doc Jim and the fresh Greek fruit dealer and the cranky conductor. They realize that Old Hank has a good heart and doesn't mean anything by vigorously and ingeniously insulting every third person who enters the store. They even tell how charitable Hank is—though they are vague about the people to whom he has been charitable. Hank becomes a tradition; his customers are a little proud of his cleverness in imitating a snarling dog.

But when you travel, particularly when you autohobo into new country, when you first behold Old Hank and do not know that he has a good heart but only that he has a bad face and a dirty store, you realize that his neighbors are too forgiving; that if they joined in one cyclonic howl they would have more fun and much cleaner groceries—or else Old Hank would retire to his proper place beside the sawdust box at the county poor farm.

Haberdasher Rampant

It is the faith of many writers on merchandising that if you just leave them alone discourteous merchants will ruin themselves. But the fact is that if a man happens to have a store well located, without too much competition near by, and if no one takes the trouble to start a crusade against him, he can get away with almost anything for years. One of the dirtiest and worst-arranged drug stores—with one of the laziest proprietors in all the Union—has for years kept alive because the store is a few blocks nearer to several large apartment houses than any other. As a bonus on his really remarkable sloppiness and pokiness the proprietor charges more for everything than the clean, efficient stores in the business center. The blame isn't really his—it belongs to the people who endure him.

Most of my examples I found along the road in motoring. But the best one I found in New York. He was the prize example of reducing disturbances by customers during business hours to a minimum.

He was a haberdasher with sandy whiskers and gravelly eyes. He had—he has—been a merchant for more than forty years; he is still in business; he is the proprietor and boss; and he knows less about the elements of salesmanship than a boy could learn in one hour. He has a one-man shop, which has never grown. I know why.

Seven years ago I went into his shop with the vague but hopeful intention of buying a tie. Anyone not actually a paranoiac knows that in this peculiar state of mind the victim hasn't any clear idea of what he wants. He'd like—oh, maybe something in blue; but—well, let's see. If he does find something which pleases him in color, design, fabric, size and price he will buy it with joy. That is the obvious reason why ties are displayed in large numbers on convenient racks. He must be caught.

This time I was not caught. I feebly spun the tie racks and paused over various spotty and wriggly and barred atrocities. All this while the proprietor—who was also day-clerk, bookkeeper and, I suspect, the porter and delivery man—regarded me with that cold sandy eye and that hot sandy outbreak of whiskers. He let me know how acidly he despised my fumbling indecision.

I hinted diffidently: "Sorry. Doesn't seem to be anything I want."

He spoke—he spoke as a dyspeptic office manager would speak to an ink-spilling office boy.

"Well, exactly what kind of a tie do you want?"

"I don't know—something a little different from anything I have now."

His voice rose till it resembled the sound of a circular saw starting to cut into a log of pine.

"If you will tell me what kind of a tie you want I'll send and get it for you. You can't expect me to be a mind reader."

I went away from that store and I never reentered it, though for two of those years I lived four blocks nearer to his shop than to any other in New York. It was a pleasure to walk the extra four blocks, even through February slush, in order not to patronize him. I had discovered why his shop had never grown; why when other haberdashers expanded from one shack to three or four palaces he remained dry and sandy, unhappy and unprosperous in a hole in the wall, pathetically trying to dress his inadequate windows with his insufficient stock, toiling to attract customers—and then to drive them out.

Conceive what he demanded when he asked me to describe exactly the kind of tie I wanted. I am not a fabric expert; like most males. I know two kinds of tie materials: "I guess this is silk" and "I don't believe this is silk." All I should have had to do in order to satisfy his request would have been to take ten years off and master the details of pattern designing, silk weaving, the chemistry of color and neckwear manufacture. Then it wouldn't have required more than a month to sit down and invent a tie and sketch it for him. Of course I should have had to give the exact color and the size to a hair's breadth of every stripe, because the difference of an inch in breadth, the difference of five per cent in the amount of red in a brown dye, would have changed the entire effect. It would be easier to describe the Grand Lama's palace without having visited Tibet.

He Kept His Shirt On—the Shelves

And if I had done all this the haberdasher would have been willing—oh, not to produce the tie from his stock, of course, but to send for it.

The larger number of haberdashers know all this. They take it for granted that if their stock does not attract the better-natured customer they lose the sale. But here was a man gray in business who did not know it—and who ragingly resented my being so peculiar as to resemble ninety-nine per cent of his trade. With a chilly indifference he watched years of perfectly good purchasing walk out of the shop.

If he were unique he would be merely a curiosity. But I have met his brothers.

Six years after this I was in the neighborhood again. I needed a couple of shirts. I hadn't time to go elsewhere and I was interested to discover whether he had learned anything. I hastened into his shop—and had exactly the same experience. I did get a dress shirt, though it wasn't what I wanted. He let me have it with only slight grudging. But when it came to choosing a negligee shirt, when after looking over his rather scant stock I could find nothing that suited me, he turned on me contemptuously and croaked: "Well, if I can't suit you I better go out of the shirt business entirely!

I hinted that this was a thing that might happen with advantage. I tried an experiment. The time before I had gone out silent, but now I wanted to see whether a man who had been in business for forty years — in New York — really could be as much of a fool as he seemed. I explained to him why it was impossible to choose out of a stock all of which displeased me any one item that would very hugely please me.

I suggested that even if I was as unreasonable as he thought it was not his business to tell me so; it was his business to welcome me.

I managed — this once at least — not to be angry.

But he turned his back on me with a bored "I guess I can run my business without your help."

That was a good, clever, satisfying and not too shockingly original thing for him to say, and despite all my efforts during this past year I don't really suppose it has cost him more than thirty or forty customers.

I asked other people in that part of town — each section of New York is a village to itself — what their experiences with this man had been. They were like my own. My friends promised to walk the four blocks farther to the better-natured and, of course, more completely stocked dealer.

I wonder how many merchants long to have such active enemies — how many of them have unconsciously created them.

This man would have succeeded in his ambition of going bankrupt but for one thing. There are many hotels, many transients, near his shop. They go to him — once. They keep him alive — barely alive. He remains there, a spider in a poor little web, a sour stomach of business, ignorant of the pleasure of doing business with friends, regarding himself as a bluff hero but to others seeming a pitiful suicide.

It is in the matter of food more than in rudeness or dishonesty that, the autohobo sees commercial inefficiency. The motorist's feeling is that he who steals my pliers steals a chunk of rust, but he who feeds me vitriol for coffee takes from me all the alimentary canal that I have.

The astonishing thing is what communities permit in the way of bad publicity. A town will spend hundreds in entertaining important visitors, thousands in getting conventions, tens of thousands in coaxing factories, all for good publicity, in the hope of enlarging the town. Yet these visitors come more or less unwillingly. In the crowding and hustle of a convention the delegates cannot see much of Bingburg—and they want to advertise their own towns.

Meanwhile Bingburg is not only neglecting but actually antagonizing a class of visitors who do want to see the town, who are not crowded and hustled, the motor tourists. And they are in fair proportion people of commercial importance. There are few financiers, executives, planners of large activities, who have not taken many motor tours and been irritated by the very towns which at a convention time would have killed them with excessive flattery.

They drive into Bingburg uninvited, requiring no coaxing, no agitated and crafty letters from the secretary of the chamber of commerce. They get out of their cars desiring to love the town. And half an hour later they go away knocking! They are not asking for gifts, for large banquets and three-color souvenirs suitable to chucking in the waste basket; they ask merely for the chance to buy decent coffee and a steak; and a bored hotel clerk yawns at them, a weary cook reaches for the frying pan—and one more important executive is ready to join in the howl of fury when Bingburg is mentioned up in the city.

I drove at nightfall into an Ohio city of twenty or thirty thousand, with a number of factories, excellent railroad connections and a violent ambition to grow. Above a store on the central square was a large electric sign, "Welcome to Anonym."

Think of that! The chamber of commerce had lavished that attention on me. I could stand on Main Street and look right up at the sign any time and realize what a homy, hospitable town this was.

Not Welcome to a Square Meal

At the hotel the clerk said sourly: "Nope, not serving any meals. Can't get the help."

"Where can I get dinner then? "

"Oh, I dunno—suppose you might try Bumbler's."

"That the best place in town?"

"Oh, I suppose so."

Bumbler's would have been a credit to any town of two hundred if it had had better cooking and service. It was a patent-sugar-bowl and not-responsible-for-hats restaurant. It had a long, pink, printed, fly-specked menu of things that were always "just out," and pinned to it a handwritten menu of things that—most unfortunately—were not out. My waitress was a thick, cheerful person with a gratuitously transparent near-silk waist. She leaned on the back of my chair and chewed gum so happily, so whole-heartedly that I could scarcely hear the electric fan or even the flies.

After a year, though I have forgotten what kinds of factories Anonym has and its advantages in railroad connections and natural gas, I remember the soggy squash, the wood-fiber string beans and the moist smack of the waitress's gum as she coyly leaned closer to my twitching ear.

I am a mild writer. I have no factories to establish, no branch offices to open. But if I had been the president of a billion dollar corporation—and I have seen such persons who are even meeker and more polite to hotel clerks and more grateful for decent Lima beans than I am myself—I should have had to dine at that same restaurant; I should have carried away the same resentment and the same eagerness never by any chance to do anything for Anonym; and if there had ever been a choice between that town and its neighbors for a new enterprise I should have been charmed to have helped to rid the earth of Anonym and all its waitresses forever.

Next morning my resentment was increased. By accident I found an excellent little cafeteria hidden away in an arcade. If the expensively maintained electric sign had announced, "Welcome to Anonym—and you can find edible food at the Soanso Cafeteria," or if the mealless hotel had told me to go there, then I should have liked Anonym; I should have believed that they cared for strangers.

Doubtless the town has a commercial club which wistfully tries to take factories away from Cleveland and Akron, from Lima and Canton. Doubtless they court strangers at conventions and give them dinners and motor rides. But in between the club permits itself to be officially represented by the stalwart gum wielder and the bored hotel clerk as guides and greeters.

I admit that one good meal would not cause a factory owner to move to town. But it would have as much, effect on him as a booklet showing in sepia the Union High School and residence of Hathaway L. Blimp. I admit that it would not be practicable to stop every foreign car costing more than X dollars—curiously enough X dollars is the exact price of the car you have just bought—and snatch open the side curtains and inquire: "Beg pardon, is there anyone in this party who is important? Ah, you? Kindly fill out this card with name, address, credit rating and official position and the secretary of our club will be charmed to take you home to lunch and try to sell you the idea of All for Anonym and Anonym for All."

Wanted: Autohobo Hotels

This rather alarming means of attack being questionable, it may some day occur to some commercial-club secretary that it would be worth while to make sure that every motor tourist is received, if not with undesired hot handshakes, at least with much-desired hot food.

If commercial clubs and city councils cannot procure perfect garages, gas stations, restaurants, hotels, let them at least make sure that strangers are not by unusually dishonest, filthy or boorish treatment sent out as violent enemies. If they can do nothing else, let them subsidize — directly or otherwise — the good dealers and warn the bad ones. Certainly let them not leave this duty of theirs to strange and furious motorists from over the state border. Or if they are too busy to do anything let them at least not add insult to injury. Let them remove from the exits from town the sign: "Good-by — come again."

The motorist is more than angelic if — when he is aching with decomposed cabbage and celluloid potatoes — he doesn't stop at that sign and thunder: "Not if I can help it!"

Somewhere in these states there is a young man who is going to become rich. He may be washing milk bottles in a dairy lunch. He is going to start a chain of small, clean, pleasant hotels, standardized and nationally advertised, along every important motor route in the country. He is not going to waste money on gilt and onyx, but he is going to have agreeable clerks, good coffee, endurable mattresses and good lighting; and in every hotel he will have at least one suite which, however small, will be as good as the average room in a great modern city hotel. He will invade every town which hasn't a good hotel already and at present that means something more than forty per cent of all towns under twenty thousand. When he has completed his work he will be in the market for European chateaux as fast as retiring royalties have to give them up.

He will find ready for his reconstruction one of the few businesses which are but little standardized. There are chain groceries, cigar stores, hardware stores, drug stores; and the shops which do not belong to a chain carry standard, nationally advertised goods. In a garage he has never seen before the motorist knows the tires which are for sale. Even doctors, farmers, lawyers, clergymen — through their associations — to some extent standardize their work and fees. And the good hotel men meet and read hotel journals.

But the bad hotels are standardized in only one thing—the two chairs in the ladies' parlor are invariably upholstered in granite cunningly carved and colored to resemble green velvet.

The new genius of country hotels is going to have an easy victory when he arrives and every autohobo from coast to coast will be his unpaid advertising man.

An Inclined Mattress

If there had been one of these chain hotels within thirty miles of us my wife and I would have driven on to it and not have stopped at a town between Spokane and Seattle which may be called Dingleville. We wobbled in after a day of dust and bumping. The hotel office was decorated in newspapers and overshoes. The bedroom—and it was the only unoccupied one in the town—was composed of four walls, practically complete, ceiling with sections of plaster removed to show what good honest work the lathers had done, a bureau which stood on one ear, a bed which indicated that more door mats were needed down at the front door, and a pitcher of water a quarter filled with sediment.

The bathroom was off the kitchen, where the hotel staff was entertaining her gentleman friend, who was convulsed by the sneaky appearance of a tall, thin, embarrassed autohobo trying to look invisible in a blue bath robe.

The mattress had a curious conformation—or it may have been geared to an eccentric. The moment I went to sleep I dropped down and over so that I almost always hit the floor seven inches forward of the footboard.

For that room we were charged two dollars. If a billiard table at a good hotel is worth four dollars for a night's sleep during convention time, then on that basis the room in Dingleville was worth forty cents.

In this hotel, as in Anonym, there was no dining room. We were warmly commended to the Bijou Restaurant, three mud puddles and a tin can away from the hotel. At the Bijou we had a breakfast consisting—where are the scientists who say there are no substitutes for eggs? The Bijou's boiled eggs were made of a substitute composed of ninety per cent of lukewarm alkali water, three per cent sulphur, and seven per cent salt.

The coffee was cold. We foolishly mentioned that fact to the waitress.

She groaned, "Well, upon my word—"

She furiously took our cups out to the kitchen and returned with hot coffee—five minutes after we had finished the eggs.

Then there was the hotel in a fairly large town in Virginia where the office had not been swept for at least a week. The proprietor sat with his feet up in a chair and told me how hard he found it to get help. It did not occur to him that he could possibly sweep the office himself. He was a sweet, clean, perfectly moral man—and he didn't live at his own hotel. He was sensible. He had a house as far away as possible.

There was the town of over a thousand near the Ohio-Indiana line, where the only hotel was a series of rooms above a bakery. To reach them you stumbled over an ancient, odorous pile of trunks and old mattresses.

There was the room in Iowa which was ventilated only by a shaft from the men's wash room. And there was the restaurant—

The proprietor must have been religious. On the wall was a sign: "If the Lord came now, would you want to have Him find you doing what you are doing?"

What I was doing was flinching before juiceless boiled beef and tasteless vegetables associated under the fraudulent firm name of "regular dinner."

The wall placard roused me. I summoned the proprietor, and not at all sacrilegiously but with high ethical purpose inquired: "Look here, if the Lord came now, do you think I'd want Him to find me ruining the good digestion He gave me by eating filth like that?"

Adventures in Autobumming

The proprietor answered, only: "Never have I had anybody kick before."

If that was true, the fault wasn't his but that of his customers. Gentle, patience is not the attitude to take toward dietetic homicide.

The two things which I am bewailing, discourtesy and bad food, were splendidly combined at a station lunch room in a big Eastern city, where I heard the Montenegrin counter waiter insult seven customers in succession.

At one fragile old woman he bawled: "If you wanted sugar in your coffee, why didn't you say so when you ordered it?"

Yet I don't know that this foreign despot was worse than the owner of the Yankee lunch room that was so filled with the fumes from a frying pan engaged in the preparation of short orders and short lives that we could not get ourselves through the cloud of smoke from the kitchen but drove on fifteen more miles, dinnerless.

If I named that town or the others the local patriots would counter by snorting: "What do you expect? New York service in a burg of five hundred?"

Why not, so far as courtesy and good food go? Not hors-d'oeuvres but at least decent beef and beans. The meanest of these towns has excellent vegetables at hand. It is the cook and the great American frying pan which turn good raw materials into poison—and for the crime of ignorance there is no excuse in the smallness of one's town. There is no known ratio between population and ability to read recipes. And sometimes it is the largest cities that have the worst cooking. But there's always an excuse. In a large urban hotel—they're too busy to take care. In a village inn—they haven't enough trade to afford a chef.

I would ardently recommend to a large number of able-bodied authoritative male lunch-room proprietors, who have been lucratively cooking for thirty years, that they learn to cook. To my warmer friends and classmates among them I tenderly urge that they forsake that frying pan which is the symbol and cause of the honored American pastime, having indigestion.

A famous chef wailed to me: "In this city there is no more home cooking. The wife goes to the movies and at fifteen minutes to six she comes home with a steak and then zh-h-h-h-h-h-h-h on the fire—and dinner is ready at six." Increasingly, with equal lack of domestic help and willingness to work, a minute's frying and ten hours in digesting take the place of cookery, and people who have become used to such barbarism at home do not complain when they encounter it at hotels.

A Race of Fryers

Fried steaks—fried pork chops—fried Hamburg steak—coarse fat chunks of fried bacon—hash fried to solidity—fried sausage meat—fried potatoes—scrambled eggs black with grease from the pan—griddle cakes prepared in the pan as often as on a griddle—these offspring of the frying pan make up the bulk of the menu in a large share of homes, and consequently in most small hotels and almost all short-order lunch rooms. The arts of baking, broiling, roasting, toasting, the use of the casserole, tend to become unknown.

The defense is the lack of assistance and the cost of fuel, but it is not enough to excuse shortening lives by ten or twenty years. It is partly the public's fault for not precisely knowing and strenuously demanding better food in these incredible restaurants along the way. And it is partly the fault of laborious but ignorant cooks. And it is partly the fault of the managers.

In many small hotels the bad food is directly traceable to the wives of the proprietors, who are the housekeepers and not infrequently the cooks. But behind that fault is that of the omnipotent male. Wife is behind the scenes, doing her best, trying to be cook, waitress, chambermaid, purchasing agent and charming spouse all at once. Husband is out in front at the desk having a perfectly wonderful time, chatting to traveling men and revolving his fingers with the armhole of his waistcoat an axis—a practice pretty to behold but not of much lasting moral value.

It is mildly advocated that in hotels where assistance cannot be obtained, where the wife is overworked, where five minutes of frying seems only too much attention to devote to cookery, the amiable father of the resort go back, read an effeminate cook book and do a little work, even at the cost of not hearing the red-hot new one from Chicago.

And it is less mildly advocated that the touring motorist, who does know good food give up his patient tolerance and explain the beauties of labor to the proprietor. The first dozen howlers will be greeted with indignation and the suggestion that "if you don't like our accommodations, you know what you can do." But the next hundred will begin to make an effect. And if thousands—and thousands—and thousands of eloquent, brilliant, brazen, violent roarers keep up the work for years and years and years it may be possible that several erring proprietors will in pathetic astonishment consider: "Why, I don't believe they like my place. Can it be just possible that even I do not know all the things in the world? Can it be actually imaginable that I, who have been so pleasantly failing at keeping hotel these twenty years, am not really the genius that, of course, I really am?"

Join the O. C. K.

When the Order of Corrective Kickers has obtained better food, which ought to be perfectly easy to do during the next two centuries, it might turn to dirty offices, uncomfortable chairs, stained wall paper, banging staircases, creaky beds, mirrors which do not mirror, naked electric bulbs so ingeniously arranged that they can be used neither for reading in bed nor for dressing, and the odor of food that is dead but not forgotten. These could most of them be remedied by the proprietor himself, and at small cost—if he knew anything.

Once in a small Florida inn frequented by hunters I heard mighty argument between a sportsman and the owner. The hunter objected to the vocal furniture. The owner said it was not remediable. The hunter borrowed a wrench and screw driver. He turned his bed and bureau on their heads, he tightened bolts and screws and in seven minutes he had killed a family of squeaks which had irritated guests for years.

He has received the Medal of the Order of Corrective Kickers, with two palms.

The existence of large automobile associations is now making it possible to kick effectively, even outside of one's town. The official of one told me what his organization had done to a thriving grafter in one of the Carolinas. They had a report from a member that he had found a puncture as he entered a town in the evening. The garage man was also the owner of the hotel. He took an hour to repair the puncture. When the driver inquired the way to a larger place ten miles beyond, the garage man insisted: "Pretty late to go on now. You couldn't find it by night. Better stay here. Good hotel."

The motorist went on. As he left the garage he wondered why the owner and his assistant were snickering. At the edge of town both of his rear tires went out. They had been slit.

He stayed at the hotel, all right—and when he returned to his own motor club, he reported. The officials telegraphed to the Carolina authorities and a few months later the enterprising garage and hotel man went to the state penitentiary.

That was scientific kicking.

But unfortunately that rudeness which is the leading motif of my symphony is not yet considered a felony and a penitentiary offense. Of course local motor clubs might correct discourtesy and merrily pass away the long winter evenings by lynching bees for rude clerks and bad cooks. But the sport has not been recognized by the athletic associations.

As to the rudeness and its psychology I had a revelation in an Illinois town of two thousand into which I drove on my way west. It is an attractive town with an excellent garage, in which the three or four mechanics strangely hold that autohobos may be human. And the principal hotel had been well planned. There was a fireplace in the office, and comfortable deep chairs and the rooms were clean. But the owner had other business interests and from six P. M. to six A. M. — precisely the time at which most travelling men and motorists arrive — he left all of the direction of the hotel to a middle-aged clerk with a whisky nose and a brandy breath.

I came in a little muddier than usual after changing a tire in a puddle and as I signed the register I inquired "What are your rates?"

The clerk superciliously glanced at the deposits of fertile topsoil on my hands and collar — oh, and probably on my ears — and reached for my key without answering my question.

I repeated it.

He sneered: "If you will kindly take the trouble to use your eyes you will note a printed schedule of prices on the wall."

In the garage across the street, I asked about the genial clerk and the entire mechanical staff stopped to laugh. They clustered about me and told stories. The clerk was the town pariah — and did not know it. His rudeness and his whiskey were traditions. No man ever stopped to hail him to "pass the time of day with him." Corner gangs winked at one another when he went by.

"Poor devil. I'm sorry f or him. No wonder he's soured," I protested.

"Him? That guy was born sour. You shouldn't fret a lot over being sorry for him. He doesn't even know people don't like him. You couldn't get through his hide with dynamite. He thinks he's such a wiz that he couldn't imagine folks making fun of him. He's the biggest bag of pink wind between Dixon and Valpo. Say, it's too bad! We've got a good hotel here, but the traveling men hate that grouch so that they'll catch a way freight to skip staying here overnight."

His Aim to Displease

It was to this man that the owner had intrusted his hotel!

I watched him all evening. A woman came down to complain that there were no towels in her room. Self-possessed, bleak, level-eyed, he looked at her and remarked quietly: "That's not my fault. Towels are put in every room every morning. What did you do with them?"

A traveling man asked the local time of an important train.

The clerk said evenly: "You will find it in the train guide on the desk."

Staying for the night was a youngster, a boy of perhaps sixteen, obviously traveling by himself for the first time in his life and excited over it with a gossipy, fluttering, confidential thrill. He went the rounds telling the older men what a corking time he was going to have in Clinton and the train he was going to take next day and just how many handkerchiefs he had in his suitcase. They stopped their writing to listen; they smiled at one another and dreamed of their own first trips.

The clerk sat alone, comfortably smoking. No one cared to talk to him, which suited him exactly. He was too superior a person to mingle with common travelers.

The boy raced up to him and panted: "Say, what time do we have breakfast in the morning?"

The clerk yawned, picked up a magazine, looked at a picture, glanced up at the boy and snorted, "Whertuknsyksskdm," or something like it.

"I—I didn't quite get you, cap'n."

The clerk closed the magazine, unable any longer to endure these outrageous interruptions to his nervous duties of rocking and smoking and reading detective stories. He spoke with a precise, controlled, chill viciousness:

"I have just told you that breakfast is served from six to eight-thirty. If you can't understand people the way they talk here in the city you better go back to the farm."

The boy wilted away. His fun in travel was gone.

I considered a project of bouncing the andirons on the

clerk's head. But being foolish I was still charitable. Perhaps there was dark history here. It was evident that the man was soaked in whisky. Perhaps he came from a fine old family — i.e., a family which unlike yours or mine is descended from the Stone Age. Perhaps he had held large positions and gone the booze path and was resentful of his fall to a petty clerkship. I wanted to get his story.

I got it at midnight, when the office was quiet and the clerk so tired of reading that he was willing to talk even to an autohobo who palpably was nobody at all.

The World His Backyard

He was descended from a fine old Kentucky saloonkeeper, and he had been a hotel clerk all his days. But, oh, he'd seen life! He wasn't, he boasted, "a darn hick, like the folks in this burg." He'd lived in Louisville and Columbus; he knew an actress, and a distiller who had a famous string of horses. He was not as other men.

"Must be kind of hard, having to handle these cranky hotel guests."

He dropped his magazine with a bang. He sat up. Here at last was one who despite the mud on his ears had the brain and soul to understand him.

"It is! You wouldn't hardly believe me if I told you how unreasonable people are. Always kicking — blaming me for everything that every wop chambermaid does. And the things they expect a fellow to know! They keep bothering me all evening with fool questions — that is, they used to bother me, but I know how to handle 'em now. I beat 'em to it. I don't take nothing off nobody. You know, you auto tourists are the worst of all — lot of you people from hick burgs coming in here and trying to let on that you're a bunch of Chicago dudes. But that guff don't go with me. Why just this morning —

"There was a fool shemale here with her husband and when they come down to pay their bill the hen spoke up and she said: 'You didn't call us at five this morning, the way you promised.' Well I just looked her square in the eye and I said: 'My dear madam, I'm perfectly aware of that interesting fact. I haven't got round to it yet. I have had other things to do.' Of course I'd been asleep, but you know how it is—don't ever let 'em get the idea they can ride you. So I never batted an eye. I let her have it straight. I says to her: 'I been busy, but I shall be through soon and if you care to go back to your room and wait I'll call you in due time!'

"Oh, I had her wild, and her husband looked sore as a crab. But Lord, he was a little sawed-off shrimp and I just gave 'em the eye and they sneaked off, and I bet they won't try to do the hoop-te-doodle high-and-mighty next time they come back here."

He was right. It is extremely unlikely. It is also unlikely that the woman or her husband will ever again annoy that hotel by going to it at all. But I wish I knew how widely and vigorously they have advertised the hotel. And I wish I knew whether the hotel owner realizes how competently his night clerk is destroying the good-will and value of his property. And most and beyond all I wish that the local motor and commercial clubs comprehended the ethical value of an ably wielded fire ax. But I do not know whether it should be wielded on the pathologic clerk or on the owner who maintains him as a public nuisance.

The effectiveness of clever clerks I saw a few weeks ago in a none-too-good hotel in an Eastern city, where the guests put up with faults in service and equipment—and price—because the chief day clerk was so cheerfully courteous and seemed at least to try to make things right.

Amiability is the most important and most profitable thing a business man has to sell.

I distinctly do not wish to imply that the autohobo keeps going from one bad hotel to another. The woes I sing are merely a few interruptions to the happiness of motor wandering. To make up for them there have been hundreds of sunny hotels and charmingly served meals, even in little unexpected places. And I do not at all imply that the standards of courtesy in hotels and restaurants are lower than those in all other establishments. It is merely that the autohobo sees more of hotels and restaurants, and it is as an autohobo that I am writing.

Few trades in this country are any too famous for courtesy. We have much to give Europe; we have perhaps a heartier good-will; but we haven't better manners. Or if we have it will not hurt us to forget it; it will not seriously effeminize the average lightsome trolley conductor to be contaminated a little by effete European conventionality. A rather distinguished English journalist who has been lecturing in the country, the best and most thoughtful of good fellows, was buying cigars at a small side-street shop in New York the other day, and as the clerk slammed down the change Sir John abstractedly said "Thank you."

The clerk retorted: "What the hell you getting sarcastic about? I give you your change as quick as I could."

I haven't yet been able to decide whether the incident revealed the clerk's opinion of the way to treat customers or the way in which cranky customers treat him. I wonder if when Sir John goes back to England he may not whisper that in the land of the free he has found a tiny per cent of citizens who are not excessively agreeable to meet. But what do we care?

We ain't runnin' our business to suit no darn furrin titled snob.

Rudeness a la Casserole

Aside from hotels and restaurants, I can recall in the matter of rudeness—not from past years, but from the past couple of months—an employment agent insulting mistresses who hinted, however timidly, that they didn't care for her mangy array of cooks; a trolley conductor who bawled "Move up, will yuh?" as though his passengers were a chain gang of criminals; a negro elevator man in a New York apartment house who snarled at a woman: "Aw,

I don't have to be polite, see? Folks goes on they knees to me to get 'em apartments"; a clerk in one of a famous string of groceries who—after these two decades of campaigning against substitution—tartly kept insisting that another brand of breakfast food was "just the same" as the brand the customer wanted; and a shrill girl child in a well-known drug store who, after a customer had refused to take a fly-specked box of candy, yelled to the cashier loud enough for the customer to hear: "That poor fish don't know what he wants—he ain't got enough money to buy no candy anyway."

When there are no more strikes—that is, only two or three a day—I want the pogrom committee of the League of Kicking Customers to employ some one of pugilistic build and a tender smile and have him peacefully go about the country starting trouble. I want him to carry smart baggage and a pair of brass knuckles. I want him, when he comes into a large city hotel, to look fondly upon the clerk and ask "What are your rates?"

When the clerk carols "I've got a nice room with bath for six dollars" I want the crusader to murmur "Can't I get a room for three?"

If the clerk snaps—and at least once in six times he will snap—"Oh, if you want a cheap room I may be able to fix you up later, but you better take this one—vacant now," then I want our secret agent to look round the lobby with a large contented smile, catch the eyes of all the traveling men in sight and bellow pleasantly at the clerk: "Yes, son, I do want a cheap room. I'm a poor man, son. I'm not rich and haughty like you. We know, even without your telling us, that when you travel you always get ten-dollar-a-day rooms. We can all tell that by looking at your expensive face. But me, I want a three-dollar room and I want you to give it to me cheerfully. And I'm going to sit round the lobby considerable this evening, son, and the next time you try to sell an expensive room by sneering so's folks won't dare ask for cheap ones I'm going to amble up and coarsely kill you."

The forty per cent or so of bad hotels vitally injure the

sixty per cent of good hotels. For as a result of having found uncomfortable accommodations, each year a larger proportion of motor tourists give up hotels entirely, good and bad, and, camp by the way. In the last five years, despite the war, there has come into existence an amazing body of camping accessories for motorists.

The Doctor Unlimbers

The East with its short runs and hard-surfaced roads does not know them; but west of the Mississippi motor camps are revelations.

Aside from camping for the sake of being outdoors and camping for the sake of avoiding dubious hotels, there is camping for the sake of showing off the delightful equipment.

I used to watch the Middle Westerners get out their hunting equipment just before September first, when the law on prairie chickens and ducks went off. Hunters don't have kits for the sake of hunting—they hunt so that they may have an excuse to use their kits.

A doctor from Chicago came up to the Minnesota stubble fields with something slightly less than an express car of the most interesting junk. He made a fully equipped army division—with tanks—look like a tramp with one spare shirt button. He possessed—and on the most hesitating invitation he exhibited—rubber, hip boots for swamp wading, rubber knee boots for wet grass and rubber overshoes for muddy roads. He had a .38 rifle, a .22 rifle, a revolver, a twelve-gauge pump gun, a double-barreled hammerless shotgun intended for duck hunting and a twenty-gauge single-barreled gun intended—so far as the village in conclave could determine—for a buggy whip. He had tin shell boxes and leather lunch boxes and compasses and extremely dangerous knives and the kind of a folding seat that a king uses when he sits and heroically butchers pheasants as they are driven past him.

The village's own idea of equipment was an old ten-gauge cannon, a pocket of shells and something, on the hip. We asserted that the doctor was not merely an idiot but actually a city fellow. We were wrong. The doctor had had more joy out of gathering his treasures than he could ever drag out of freezing on any duck pass or shooting partridges he did not wish to eat. What was one wretched dead bird compared with the excitement of putting on a leather coat with eighteen trick pockets to explore.

The same applies to autobumming equipment. You can, if you put up at hotels, cross the continent with no extra equipment save a tow rope and a bag of large stones to be carefully dropped upon the backs of dogs that race along and try to bite your tires. Or you can get so much pleasure out of buying accessories that afterward you won't care whether you merely take the trip — and you certainly won't be able to afford to. Novices will find sporting and accessory shops happy hunting ground and if they have never by the scenery and the hope of freedom been tempted to autohobo they will be by the equipment.

Aside from motor access, pumps which do not cause you to break your back, magic Jacks which will raise a car with the pressure of a little finger there are tables which fold to the size of checker board, pneumatic mattresses with which you can sleep on flinty ground, elaborate tiny ranges with portable fuel. But the triumph, the thing which makes it possible to be independent of hotels when you desire or to stay at them when you are weary of picnicking is the complete camping outfit — familiar from Davenport to the Coast, almost unknown in the East and South.

It is seen in the trailer, of which there are now a dozen different makes, costing from seventy-five dollars to three hundred. The typical trailer during transportation folds to the size of a coffin on wheels, but opens out into a storm-proof tent with two real spring-and-mattress beds, a dining table between them and shelves and an ice box at the end. The trailer tents can be pitched in ten minutes and on their roller bearings and pneumatic tires they can easily be hauled.

Yet they are adequate for a two weeks' stay and make it

possible to remain as long as you like at the miraculous lake which you happen to discover.

There are smaller and cheaper outfits sufficient for a comfortable stay of one or two nights—canvas-sheltered beds with the heads resting on the running board, mud-proof, rain-proof, wind-proof. A like shelter is a cot with a tiny tent over it and a window for ventilation—and for looking out at the natives who come to inspect this new kind of bug. There are steel frames which fit on the tops of the seats and make excellent beds up under the top—and you can connect to the battery an incandescent bulb for night reading.

There is just one piece of equipment which the author urges—and it isn't patented. That is a large competent piece of cheesecloth for camping in mosquito country. I spent one night by Lake Itasca and I spent it awake—not because I was breathing in the sweet air or thinking romantically of the old voyageurs and missionary monks and of the river rolling from this pine forest down to New Orleans or any of those beautiful things that might have made a poet lie awake. I was engaged in keeping a smudge lighted; plucking long and excessively wet grass—on my knees, out in the delightful dew; poking it into a tin can which regularly tipped over and spilled the fuel; and being slowly turned into a cross between a smoked ham and a large embodied sneeze.

We had plenty of mosquito netting along, but to a north-woods no-see-um the meshes of mosquito netting are large enough to hold a war dance in.

Troubles and weariness of motoring—you must be prepared for them. But one glorious morning's run makes up for all the discomforts of a long trip. Once we drove nearly two hundred miles from the elbow of Cape Cod to Springfield, Massachusetts, before noon. It was October with the leaves turning. We left at five in the darkness. For fifty miles we did not see another vehicle, another human being. It was sheer magic, slipping through the steely air over macadam roads. Nothing could ever halt us; we flew as in a dream.

The sum burst up, its new light flashing on lacquered

leaves and the first frost of the season, which silvered the trunks and rocks and the chips in a woodland clearing. Along the sharp hill ridge we overlooked russet valleys as from an aeroplane. We came into Springfield with no sense of effort expended. Where on the train we should have been stuffy and stiff and dulled, we rode in like horsemen after a morning gallop.

That was traveling as it was meant to be—not mere getting somewhere but going for the sake of going.

And once we spent the night on the vast and open prairie between Bismarck and Dickenson in North Dakota. Awe crept over us as we sat on stools by the tent. The huge orb of the land was mightier than mountains or the ring of ocean. Here was the heart of America; and we had come here, not coaxed by hotel signs or business engagements but merely because, driving westward it had seemed a possible place to stop for the night. Carelessly, by chance, we had driven into wonderland; and as dusk drifted down and the car and tent were as insignificant as a lone wheat shock on that prairie, we forgot all the day's insignificances of dust and punctures and road finding and in that great stillness were thankful that—as only gypsies or autohobos could—we had happened upon the quiet place of the elder gods.